PARTING THE VEIL

HOW TO COMMUNICATE WITH THE SPIRIT WORLD

PARTING THE VEIL

HOW TO COMMUNICATE WITH THE SPIRIT WORLD

Stuart and Dean James-Foy

Visionary Living, Inc.
New Milford, Connecticut

Parting the Veil:
How to Communicate with the Spirit World

By Stuart and Dean James-Foy

Copyright Stuart and Dean James-Foy, 2017

Published by Visionary Living, Inc.
New Milford, Connecticut
www.visionaryliving.com

Front cover design by April Slaughter
Back cover and interior design by Leslie McAllister
Illustrations by Dai Cable, website www.daicable.com
Photography by Karley Smith-Foy

ISBN: 978-1-942157-21-2 (pbk)
ISBN: 978-1-942157-22-9 (epub)

Disclaimer: The authors and publisher accept no responsibility for the use of any practices or exercises in this book or any results that may follow. The reader accepts full responsibility for any undertakings from this book.

Stuart dedicates this book to the Goddess and God, angels, and the spirit world, whose guidance and love is with him always.

Dean would like to dedicate this book to his Mum in spirit, and to his Dad, who gave him the courage to be himself.

Together, they dedicate the book to their dear friends, Carol and John, who have sat with them in circle for nearly 20 years, sharing the wonders of spirit.

TABLE OF CONTENTS

FOREWORD
BY ROSEMARY ELLEN GUILEY

Contact with the spirit world has always been shrouded in mystery. The veil that separates the realm of the living from the realm of the dead and spirits seems immovable, except under certain conditions when gifted and skilled individuals can break through. Those who can part the veil – the mystics, seers, mediums, oracles, prophets, psychics, shamans and others – have always been sought after throughout the ages.

Few born on this earth have not pondered the afterlife, and wondered how to reach through the barrier to talk to the souls on the other side. Can anyone do it? Or just those who have 'the gift'?

The answer is yes, we all have the capability to do so. There are indeed certain persons born with the marked sensitivity and natural ability to see, hear and sense the dead and spirits from an early age. Yet, everyone is born with a measure of that same ability – and there is much that we can do to develop it into a fine psychic and mediumistic skill.

Most individuals have spontaneous contact with the dead and spirits. The contact comes through dreams, signs and synchronicities, a 'presence', and other personal ways. Such events usually serve to alleviate grief and give us evidence that the soul is immortal and carries on, and that our loved ones on the other side are aware of us and can reach out. We can gain much more, however, through the skill of mediumship, in which we open the door and invite spirit to join us in communication.

My early life psychic experiences propelled me into developing my own ability, to see if I could open the link that would yield a stream of impressions and information. I read, studied and took classes. In the process, a magnificent vista opened to me: the spirit realm!

Here now is a beautiful guidebook to make your study organized and productive. It is packed with information and easy-to-use exercises and instructional material, all designed to help your natural ability flower. Stuart and Dean James-Foy have "the gift", and they have translated their years of personal and professional experience into an introductory course that will help anyone, beginners and advanced students alike, sharpen their skills.

My husband, Joe, and I met Stuart and Dean a few years ago in Salem, Massachusetts, where I give an annual black mirror scrying event in the Halloween season. Black mirrors, as you will learn inside these pages, are modern versions of ancient tools for contacting the dead and spirits. 'Scrying' in an old Middle English term for 'describing' and 'discerning dimly'. In the event, people gaze into dark mirrors and experience contact with friends and family on the other side. It's a moving evening, and often quite emotional for many of the participants.

Stuart and Dean participated in one of these events, and in the discussion at the closing shared their personal experiences. Afterwards, we struck up a conversation. As we were all in Salem for a few days, we got together again... and the rest has become history. Over the years we have become fast friends, and we have shared all kinds of paranormal, psychic and spiritual adventures on both sides of the Atlantic. Stuart and Dean are family.

I have learned a great deal from them. I have witnessed their ability to make contact and deliver, with compassion and sensitivity, meaningful messages from departed loved ones. Stuart and Dean not only have finely developed skills, they are filled with spiritual light and a genuine desire to help others. What's more, they have a terrific sense of humor – something that is always useful in dealing with the spirit world!

Developing your mediumistic skill has many benefits besides contact with the other side. It enhances your spiritual development and in turn your daily life. It expands your awareness to the powerful energy of nature, to the energy fields that surround us and all living things, and to our connection to something greater and transcendent. Whether your goal is personal and private, or you wish to become a professional medium, this book is for you.

I am pleased to publish *Parting the Veil: How to Communicate with the Spirit World.*

Introduction

Hello and welcome to *Parting the Veil: How to Communicate with the Spirit World*. This book is designed for anyone and everyone with an open mind and open heart. You may be a total beginner wishing to delve into the wondrous world of spirit communication. Perhaps you are a seasoned practitioner, looking to bring a fresh approach to your personal practice or with your work in circle.

This book will take you on a very special journey, and by the end, you will feel a stronger connection with the spirit world. It may also help to heal grief, or alleviate feelings of worry about death and dying.

Spirit communication and mediumship have been in use since ancient times, and today they are more popular than ever. We have seen a huge increase in the popularity of this subject over the last 30 years or so, with more people consulting mediums, or knowing someone who has. Some readily tell the stories of their own first-hand experiences.

So why is spirit work so popular today? It seems more and more people are coming away from some of more traditional religious beliefs that denounce working with the spirit world. They are questioning what they have been told to believe and want to learn the truth for themselves. People seem more open-minded and savvy about spiritual and paranormal topics. They want to draw their own conclusions on the subjects. TV and radio shows, events, and a plethora of books have sparked even more interest in spirit. In return, the spirit world is delighted that more people are interested in making contact. We know, they've told us! The world of spirit reaches out in many ways, and all you need to do is want to make that connection.

So, why do people want to contact the spirit world and connect with loved ones, friends and guides? Everyone has their own personal reasons. Over the years of working, we have had this discussion with many students, and we have identified three main reasons why people embark on this journey:

- *Curiosity*. People are just curious, it's in their nature. They may have heard all about mediums and other people's wonderful experiences, but are wondering if there really is anything to it. They need proof for themselves. With an open mind, they just might get it.

- *Loss of a loved one*. Some people have been deeply affected by the passing of someone close. They need to know that there is an afterlife and that the person who has crossed over into spirit is okay, safe and happy. When contact happens under these circumstances, it provides a healing experience for those on both sides of the veil. The healing is especially powerful for persons suffering deep grief, and for those who need closure for old wounds, rifts, and disagreements. It is often a life-changing experience.

- *Attraction to work in the field*. Others feel drawn to work in the field of spirit communication. They may have had experiences since childhood. For some, their experiences begin in adulthood. These individuals feel a deep calling to develop their gifts for the betterment of mankind. You just know if you have the calling, for it is loud and clear and a truly beautiful experience.

No matter what the reasons, people pursue their spirit communication work in a variety of ways. Some do it privately to fulfil personal needs, and others are more public about it, attending spirit communication events, Spiritualist churches and development circles.

Most of us have the capacity to learn the art of mediumship. Your mediumistic ability may already be in full flourish or it may be lying dormant, waiting to be explored. All that is required, as we've noted, is an open mind and open heart. You must also 'want' to be able to develop.

Spirit communication is a natural ability that can be finely tuned with the correct training and exercises. We can develop our gifts to such a degree that we're able to get clear, concise messages from the spirit world. You can never know enough about this subject. Knowledge is empowering!

We have crafted the exercises in this book based on our years of experience as both psychic mediums and teachers. We have seen some of the most amazing results with our students using these exercises. We have seen how life-changing spirit communication can be, and the many blessings it can bring. Spirit will guide us in all that we do, and life can be so much better for it.

We share with you our personal experiences and perspectives. Some of our views may differ from other sources you have read, learned from, or consulted. Expanding your repertoire is essential for successful spirit communication, and we invite you to try new things so you can reap the rewards.

In spirit communication, there is no right or wrong – it's all about what works for you as an individual or group. Getting evidence and wisdom from the spirit world is the goal at the end of the day.

We ask you to read and practice, no matter what level of development you consider yourself. We encourage you to read the book in its entirety and gain familiarity with the contents before you embark on the exercises. This will aid you in getting the most out of your contact with the other side. Once you have read and understood what the book is about, you can dip in and out to different sections to deepen your knowledge and understanding.

We wish you many hours of magical spirit communication. Know that it will always lead you to love, light and wisdom.

Blessed Be
Stuart and Dean James-Foy
www.stuartanddean.com

CHAPTER 1

THE DOOR TO THE SPIRIT WORLD

Many individuals who are drawn to mediumship find that the door to the spirit world opens early in life, with spontaneous visions of the dead, phenomena in haunted homes, and encounters with spirits and invisible beings in nature. In general, children are more psychically open than adults, and many youngsters have unusual experiences. Sometimes their parents and other adults around them discourage such experiences, or at least won't talk about them, dismissing them as fantasy. Some children quietly find out that the adults in their families are 'seers' as well, and they are the latest in a long line of multi-generational, psychically gifted individuals. Those with an unusual gift, stronger and more marked than average, soon stand in an open doorway that reveals a mysterious and marvellous reality.

So it was with us, and we'd like to share a bit with you what growing up with an eye into the spirit world was like.

About Stuart

Stuart James-Foy

I was born in Sutton Coldfield, a small town in central England, in April 1978. Many people in my family have psychic gifts, and from childhood I began experiencing contact with the other side. I was so young at the time that I didn't know I was communicating with the spirit world. I just accepted what I was seeing and experiencing.

I was always told about my grandfather, who passed shortly before I was born. He was described as the most loving and gentle man. He would tell the family that he was looking forward to meeting me once I was born, but it was not meant to be.

My grandmother told me about experiences she had after his passing. She said that I, as a baby, would often interact with someone unseen in her house, and she knew her husband was around. I don't remember those earliest experiences, as I was only 1 or 2 years of age. However, I do remember back to when my experiences started when I was about 4 and 5. I would see my grandad in my grandmother's bedroom, where he had passed from cancer, and I would especially feel him strongly, whenever I stayed with her for the night.

I slept in the bed with my grandmother, which was the same bed my grandad had passed away in. I was always intrigued and amazed when I saw and felt my grandad around. He made me feel safe and loved. I never felt afraid. It was like he was there, physically. I often spoke to my grandmother about it and she would never dismiss it, but tell me that he was keeping us safe.

I had many dreams when I was younger about spending time with my grandad. I now know that these were indeed dream visitations of his spirit. I discovered much later that dream visits with the dead are a widespread phenomenon, and have been recorded since ancient times. Our dreams take us beyond the physical world, and to meeting places where we can be reunited with loved ones who have passed on. Even now I still feel like I had many great times with him, and I know that I did in spiritual truth.

By the time I got to the age of 7, I was having many spiritual and paranormal experiences in the family home. The house was a pre-war, semi-detached 1930s dwelling in the Pype Hayes area of Birmingham, England. It was quite haunted, and not by a nice presence, but a very dark force. We all would experience shadow figures, footsteps running up and down the stairs, voices coming from nowhere, and a general feeling of unrest. One family member had an incident not long after I was born in 1978. He claimed that he awoke one night with the feeling of something hovering over him, and then a strong feeling of hands pressing down on his chest.

Some would say that it was only sleep paralysis, but I know that was not the case. It was a phenomenon called 'hag attack.' In earlier times, invisible presences that pressed down upon people in bed were blamed on witches – hence the term 'hag' – and also on demonic entities. The hag attack, also called the Old Hag syndrome, occurs around the world and has been recorded for many centuries. It defies the sleep paralysis explanation, and is often tied to unpleasantly haunted places, and to individuals with certain kinds of attachments. Our house evidently had a resident unfriendly spirit that was capable of attacking people while they slept.

Years later, a friend of my brother stayed overnight in the same room, not knowing about what had happened earlier. I remember him coming down to breakfast the next morning with a pale white face of what I can only describe as sheer terror. He said in the night he awoke to the feeling that someone was hovering above him and then 'something' grabbed his ankles. He was terrified, as he couldn't see anything but could certainly feel it. When the family asked how long this encounter lasted, he wasn't sure, as he was so frightened by the whole experience. He just lay there frozen with fear, but eventually the spirit moved away from him, seemingly of its own accord. He was too scared to get out of bed once the experience stopped, and he lay awake the rest of the early hours until sunrise, when he felt it was safe to get out of the room.

When I was around 8 years old, I had a neighbour friend, Louise, who lived across the street. Louise was a couple of years older than me but we got on very well. One day I went to Louise's house as usual to play games and have a laugh, as you do at that age. As a child, my circle of friends all seemed to be interested in ghost stories and the paranormal. We would often watch the TV series *Arthur C. Clarke's World of Strange Powers,* which talked about all things paranormal, especially ghosts and spirits. We had heard about séances and had seen an episode about 'messages from the dead', so in true style, around seven of us decided to gather in Louise's garage to try a séance out for ourselves. It was a dark day and very wet, so it seemed like the perfect time.

The garage was mostly dark inside with just a shaft of light coming through a small frosted window of the garage door, just enough for us to see each other. We sat in a circle and linked hands. Louise said we should hold our hands higher, about shoulder height, as the spirits preferred that. To this day I don't know where that came from, but it seemed right at the time. On her recommendation, we did just that, and I was nominated to call out to any spirits to show themselves. We closed our eyes and I asked, 'Is there anybody there?' We sat still with bated breath.

Suddenly, there was a loud cracking noise like electricity in the garage and we all felt a jolt of energy running through us. It was strong enough for us to break contact with our hands and we stood up. Two girls were crying and shaking, saying they had seen a man with a crooked walking stick. I saw this figure too, just at the moment of the cracking sound. (I now know this was the sound of a strong spirit making his presence known.) I was shaken, but so intrigued that I needed to know more about what I had just experienced. Was it spirit communicating with us? Deep down I knew it was and this excited me. The séance ended there as we all seemed to be a little weary after this experience. I tried to initiate another séance, but none were willing to try again, except for me.

Louise's family started emptying their attic. A few weeks after our amazing contact in the garage, her father came down from the attic, having cleaned the last few boxes out of the space. He had a wry smile on his face, a combination of humour and nervousness. He was carrying a thin box under his arm that looked like a board game – Monopoly, perhaps? But no, her father presented me and Louise with a tatty box. It had the name 'William Fuld' printed on it and underneath in capital letters 'OUIJA'.

I immediately knew what this device was. I had seen one at another friend's house before. I was an unusual child in that Ouija boards didn't scare me, but intrigued me.

Louise's father said to us, 'Have you seen this? Do you know what it is?' His tone was disapproving but he put the box down on the coffee table and walked away. Louise was not up for using the board, but I was. I asked if I could take it home, and without hesitation Louise said yes.

My mum was not happy with this 'thing' brought into her house but turned a blind eye to it. She was aware, as we all were, of the spirit that resided in the house with us. I thought that maybe now we would finally get some answers about this unseen entity. I want to stress here that the Ouija board did not bring or invite the spirit into the house. This dark entity was already there and was waiting for the opportunity to connect with us.

My brother, who was 6 years older than me, was also very intuitive (he'd been reading Tarot for a couple of years). He was instantly all in and wanted to use the board with me. We sat in his bedroom with the Ouija placed on our knees, as we felt it would have a stronger connection to us. We placed our hands on the dusty planchette. We asked, 'Is there anybody there?' and were thrilled when the planchette slowly began to move. A tingle of excitement raced through my body and we looked at each other in amazement. 'Are you pushing it?' we asked each other. The planchette answered quickly for us as it shot to the word 'NO'.

We made contact with someone who went by the name of 'Mrs. Ford', who said she had died there. We asked, 'Did you die in the house?' She said, 'No'. Then came the word that no one wants to hear... 'murdered'. It brought that session to an abrupt end. My brother and I felt nervous about what the Ouija had just imparted.

Back in the 1980s we had no internet, so you couldn't just Google for more information. As savvy kids and fans of *Scooby-Doo,* we decided to ask a lovely old couple who had lived opposite our house for years. Mr. and Mrs. Austin were a friendly couple in their seventies. We approached the house and knocked on the door. Mr. Austin came to the door first, followed by his wife.

'We have a question we would like to ask you', said my brother.

'Ok, what would you like to know'? Mr. Austin replied.

'Do you know of anyone called Mrs. Ford who lived in our house?'

They looked at each other perplexed and said, 'No'. We were disappointed until Mr. Austin added, 'I'm sure she lived in the adjoining house and died many years ago'.

We were surprised, but also pleased to hear confirmation of what we had been told via the Ouija. Was it indeed Mrs. Ford's spirit in the house returning to places that seemed familiar?

We soon learned this was not the case.

We told the Austins of the ghostly activity that was occurring in the house. They listened to us with respect but finished by saying a few words which I will never forget: 'If we told you what happened in that house, you'd never sleep in there again.' We pleaded with them to elaborate, but they said no and that we were too young to know. They politely excused themselves and left me and my brother pondering about the possibilities.

We thought perhaps a murder or suicide had taken place, but after visiting the local library and checking the microfiche, we found nothing.

Weeks went by and the activity in the home increased in frequency and intensity. It was noticed by all the inhabitants, including our dear cats, who for one week refused to enter the kitchen to eat. They appeared to feel a cold spot and a very negative presence in the kitchen. Even during cooking, when the room should naturally heat up, it would stay icy cold. After a week, the cold spot went away and the cats happily returned there for food.

We started seeing shadows all over the house, not just out of the corner of the eye, but also right in front of us. My mum tried to play down on the activity so not to frighten us. One day my brother and I decided to take photos in the house to see if we could capture a picture of the spirit. We walked around the house and snapped photos with a slim 110 film camera. We asked, 'If there is a spirit here, please show yourself now'. We would then take the photo.

When we finished taking the shots we went to the local pharmacy to have the film developed. We got the photos back and excitedly opened the packet. We began looking through them, but each print bought disappointment as nothing seemed to be showing… until the last few photos.

A photo taken of the living room clearly showed a cowled figure standing by the dark brown curtains. It had a distorted skull-like face and bony hands, and seemed to be wearing a cloak of some kind. It sounds cliché but that's what was there. One other photo that was taken at the bottom of the staircase showed the same figure, except this time it seemed to be kneeling, with what looked like rosary beads around its

7

neck. These photos blew us away and proved that what we were sensing and experiencing was indeed very real.

We showed our mum the prints and she freaked out, instantly ripping them up and destroying the negatives. I was gutted and still am to a degree, as the photos were some of the most amazing evidence I have seen of phantom photography. I understand her reasoning and know she was frightened. She refused to ever mention them again.

I knew by this time that the presence in the house was a dark and mean-spirited creature. It would prowl the house night and day. We would hear footsteps going up and down the stairs.

One Saturday, my brother and I were at home watching the TV when suddenly an almighty crash came from upstairs. We jumped up ready to have a look when we heard heavy footsteps in our mum's bedroom above the living room. The ceiling light was vibrating with each loud footstep.

The footsteps started making their way downstairs. We ran over to the door to hold it shut, assuming somehow an intruder had got in the house. The footsteps continued along the hallway and we could feel the vibration on the floor boards as 'it' got closer to the door. We had our ears pressed to the door, hearts thumping, and heard the presence move in to the kitchen, walking on the quarry tiled floor. Then we heard the back-door handle rattle, and then silence. Our hearts were pounding not knowing who, or what, was there.

I knew it was the spirit and it was showing us its power. After 10 minutes of silence we felt brave enough to explore and tentatively opened the living room door. After inspection, we could see that the back door was indeed locked and bolted. Slowly we climbed the stairs to look around, starting in Mum's room. On entering the bedroom, we found what had caused the great crashing sound. The dressing table in the bay window had been tipped over and all the ornaments and hairbrushes from the top were strewn across the floor.

A few weeks later, still trying to capture evidence, we placed a tape recorder in the house whilst we all went shopping, whilst the house was empty. On returning, we found that a holy statue of the Blessed Virgin Mary that had been placed on the windowsill at the top of the stairs by my brother was now in pieces at the bottom of the stairs – not just broken, but smashed to pieces like something had thrown it with force. The tape had stopped recording by that time, as tape recorders back then only ran for a short time. We listened to the tape and all was quiet until we heard loud birdsong. It was not coming from outside, as it was loud and sounded close to the built-in microphone. Then we heard a female voice say, 'Mum, mum'.

Things came to a head after this experience. The activity increased to an almost daily occurrence, and the tension in the house was tangible. The activity ranged from footsteps, loud bangs, shadows and the feeling of a negative presence. What else could possibly happen, we wondered?

Unbeknownst to the rest of us, my brother was upstairs in his bedroom one night using the Ouija alone, something I would never advocate. I was downstairs with my mum when we heard an almighty scream. My brother flew down the stairs looking terrified. He said he heard a noise that sounded like a chip bag rustling and crunching whilst he was using the board. He looked up and saw a huge spider, like a tarantula – a rare thing in cold old England.

We giggled and made our way upstairs to investigate, expecting to find a common house spider. I will never forget what I saw, and it still makes me shiver to this day. It was indeed a jet black, tarantula-sized spider hanging upside down from the ceiling. We screamed and ran to a neighbour, Tony, who lived up the road. He said he would get it for us.

Tony was a big guy and not easily frightened. He walked into the bedroom and then doubled back on himself, saying, 'I'm not going near that'! We pleaded with him and finally he said, 'I'll be back in a minute'. He went back to his house and returned wearing gloves and a long-sleeved top with duct tape wrapped around the gloves to prevent the spider from going down his sleeves. He grabbed it off the ceiling and it writhed in his hand. He took it outside and stamped on it, something to this day I don't agree with, but he was fearful that it was poisonous. I've never seen any spider that size in England and never want to again.

The next day, my brother tried to burn the Ouija board but it didn't burn. Maybe it was made of a material that wouldn't burn, or maybe there was something else behind its apparent invincibility to fire. He broke it up into pieces and a neighbour put it into an incinerator at his place of work.

After a few months, my brother acquired another board, explaining that he said he felt lost without one. By this time, I was living at my grandmother's house for a couple of years because of family unrest, unrelated to the haunting, and so I did not use the board with him. One day my mum came to see me at my grandmother's house, which was just two blocks away, around the corner from our haunted house. Suddenly, my brother came running up my grandmother's garden pathway, out of breath and terrified. Excuse the pun, but he was as white as a ghost.

He burst through the front door, unable to speak. Once he got his breath back, he told us that he had been chased from the house by the negative entity. He said he had been clearing his bedroom and had decided to get rid of this second Ouija board. He decided to throw it onto the stairs landing ready to dispose of it. As he bent down to pick it up, from the corner of his eyes he saw an apparition run from our mum's bedroom and stand at his side. He saw the legs of the entity and felt that the presence was unhappy at the thought of the board being disposed of. As he ran down the stairs, he could feel the entity swirling around him. He shut himself in the living room hoping the entity would stay outside. He saw my mum's cigarettes on the mantel piece and lit one. He was only around 16 years old, but his experience terrified him to the point that he lit a cigarette to help calm his nerves.

After five minutes or so he felt a little calmer – until the presence entered the living room where he was seeking refuge. This time he did not see it, but felt such anger emanating from it as it entered the living room through a closed door. My brother knew he had to get out of the house, so he made a break for it and ran out, leaving all the doors open. It was then that he came to my nan's house.

I remember the look on my mum's face. She tried to play it down to calm the situation, but I could tell she was fearful of what had just happened. As the house was left open, we decided to go there to see if the entity was still present, and to secure the house from any mortal intruders.

We walked around the blocks briskly and soon came to our house. We saw the net curtains twitch upstairs as if someone was peering from behind. We knew no one was inside. This is something we would see on a regular basis even when all the windows and doors were closed and the house was empty.

On entering the house, the feeling of dread was thick in the air. You could have cut the atmosphere with a knife. We were accustomed to an ongoing dense, thick and oppressive energy, but this was worse. Days went by and things seemed to become calmer. The Ouija was still in the house but was wrapped up, and prayers had been said over it. Eventually the second Ouija was broken into pieces and disposed of.

A few years went by and the activity died down. Had 'it' finally gone? Had it left us? Everyone in the house seemed to think so, but I could still feel it watching, lying dormant, waiting for its next opportunity.

Around 1992, when I was 14, my mum became romantically involved with a new man and decided to sell the house. It was only on the market a short time, as the properties sold quickly around there. The moving day came and the family were elated at finally being able to move from the house of unhappy memories. The removal guys arrived and emptied the house of its contents. I wanted to have the last look around before we left – after all, it had been my childhood home.

While the family were outside loading the last few delicate pieces into the car, I walked up the stairs and looked into the empty rooms. Suddenly, I was aware that the presence was there and growing stronger, watching and trying to intimidate me. I wasn't having any of it. I stated out loud that 'it' had lost and I was not afraid anymore. I said emphatically, 'Do not try and follow us, either'. I had very strong faith in the divine, the angels and my spirit helpers by that time. I felt safe and secure in the knowledge that I could overcome anything with their help, including this. I walked out of the house with my head held high and with a grin from ear to ear, knowing that that part of my life was over.

These experiences inspired me to do the work that I do now. Part of that work is to help families overcome troublesome hauntings and return their home to a place of happiness and peace, which every home should be. Clients appreciate that I have 'been there'. This helps them feel more at ease because they know that I came through it without any scars and that they can too. I always point out that every case is different and some can take a long while to clear. Some clients have to learn to live with their visitors on an ongoing basis, but it's all about how to deal with it as a family or occupant. There are ways to go on living and enjoying life and not become a victim of an unwanted spirit.

Spirit and the divine have continued to be a huge part of my life, helping me in other areas too. Working with them every day makes me feel so humbled. They intervened, when I was 15, saving me during a mugging incident. I was travelling to a dance class in a part of Birmingham, England. The neighbourhood was not the best but the dance school was. It was a dark winter evening around 6.30 pm.

I had taken a bus to the terminus, and the dance school was a brief five-minute walk. I was only one minute from the school when I was attacked. A big guy over six feet tall stepped out from a public phone box. He walked quickly over to me and put his arm around my shoulder. My stomach sank and knew his intentions were not good. He told me to walk down the underpass with him. I knew if I went down there with him, out of sight, all sorts of bad things could happen. I decided to make a run for it, but he grabbed the hood of my coat with such strength that it prevented me from getting away. He pushed me against some railings and grabbed me by the scruff of the neck with one hand and told me to stand still. He then slowly reached into his back pocket with the other hand. I thought, 'It's a knife', and I was terrified!

This is when I mentally asked, 'Help me, please'. I put a silent call out into the universe for a divine intervention. In an instant, I suddenly became aware of what I can only describe as a mist surrounding me. I could see it, and I knew that I was not alone and that I was being protected by all I had faith in. My terror turned to instant calm, knowing that I was going to be fine. I looked at the attacker in the eyes and as he stared back at me. Now he was not reaching in his back pocket, but had a look of confusion and uncertainty. I knew he could feel 'something' around me. He let me go and ran off, looking perplexed.

Another notable time that spirit helped me was in 2002. They intervened whilst I was driving, giving me a warning that if I hadn't heeded, I would probably not be writing this book.

I had passed my driving test in summer of 2002. I was gaining more confidence as the months were progressing. I was driving home in November of that year from a long day at work. It was a dark winter evening around 7 pm. I had just taken my turning and was approaching a traffic roundabout when out of nowhere a spirit voice said, 'Slow down'. I knew it was spirit as I was the only one in the car. As I slowed down the spirit voice then said, 'Stop'. I instantly stopped, and luckily no other car was behind me.

Just as I had stopped, to the right of the traffic roundabout came a speeding car without headlights, being chased by a police car. Now, I know that if I hadn't listened to the spirit voice, the speeding car would have ploughed into me and I would have been very badly injured or worse. I was totally taken aback and felt privileged that spirit was there for me again, to keep me safe and protected.

I have a very strong bond with the spirit world and the divine, and I believe the more people who develop their mediumistic and psychic abilities, the more enriched their lives can become.

About Dean

Dean James-Foy

How did a young lad born of Irish and English parents, raised as a Catholic, become a source for spirit contact?

I suppose my first memory goes back to when I was 3 years old. My mother, heavily pregnant with my sister, asked if I could think of a name for the baby. 'Rosy' I heard very strongly in my head. 'Rosy', I shouted back in excitement. My mother asked me to choose another name. However, Rosy kept on coming above any other names I could think of. My sister was finally name Beverley. Years later I discovered that my grandmother's name on my mother's side was, in fact, Rose, or Rosy as she liked to be called. I never knew my grandparents on my mother's side, for they had both passed before I was born. I never did forget that sweet sounding voice prompting me at such a young age.

Between the ages of 8 and 10 I can very clearly recall lying in my bed fast asleep. Nearly every night, I suddenly I found myself at the top of the very long and steep Victorian staircase that led down to our living room. I gently floated down the stairs, filled with peace and happiness. This happened many times over that two-year period. I realize now that these were my first experiences of astral travel.

Although I was raised a Catholic, I never went to a Catholic school. This resulted in me having to go to Sunday school every week. Lessons in the bible were duly taught by the nuns of the church. I was a very independent soul, even at such a young age, which didn't set me in good favour with the nuns. I was always asking, 'Why'? or 'How'? I was constantly snitched on by the nuns to my dad, who would tell me off each week. He said I was to accept what the nuns said and not ask the reason why.

This never sat comfortably with me. I remember asking one of the nuns if she believed in ghosts. 'NO', was the answer. 'But what about the Holy Ghost'? I asked. The response was, 'You ask too many questions and you should accept the teachings of Christ'. The nuns told my dad about this question I had asked. This was something my dad respected me for, and I was soon released from my Sunday school attendance.

Although through my formative years the only actual spirit voice I heard seemed to be that of my grandmother, I did have many moments of deja vu. I would arrive at a new location and have a feeling that I'd already been there before – in a previous life, perhaps? I also had the gift of knowing what was going to happen the very next minute. I never really thought much about it, as I thought this was perfectly natural to most people. This gift waned over the next few years as I headed into my late teenage years. The turning point, unbeknownst to me, was just around the corner.

I was in my early twenties, by which point I'd been to drama school and had become a professional actor. I was also very heavily involved in the local community youth theatre. It was after one of these shows that everything was brought more sharply into focus. It was around 11 pm at night. I'd just finished the run of a community theatre youth show. I was giving my colleague a lift home in my much-loved Austin Morris Mini Van, a car that I had always felt very safe and secure in. It was a dark, dry night as I drove along the unfamiliar roads of Kenilworth, a small market town in Warwickshire, a few miles from Stratford-upon-Avon. We were excitedly chatting about the show that evening. The tree-lined roads were thick with leaves obscuring the street lights somewhat, and to my harm, a give way sign.

Not realizing that I was approaching a crossroads, I continued forward without stopping. My friend screamed as a car coming full speed from the left-hand side of the road ploughed into us. Oddly enough, I still recall feeling very safe as the force of the car bent my Mini Van in two. The windscreen shattered. There were screeching sounds, the smell of burning rubber, and finally a full stop as the Mini Van embedded itself in a brick wall, which then collapsed onto parts of the van. People in a public house across the way ran out to see what they could do. I had my eyes closed and didn't want to open them, for fear of what I might see. My friend was okay but said his leg was bruised.

Blue lights and sirens broke the calm. The emergency services personnel cut the door off the passenger side so my friend could be released. While they were doing this, I slowly opened my eyes. Looking down at my hands and arms and wiggling my toes, I could see that everything seemed to be fine. I was sad that my faithful Mini Van was like a crushed can. After a while I was helped to stand out of the vehicle. That's the last thing I remember.

Next, I was in the ambulance on the way to hospital. The ambulance man was telling my friend that they usually do an on the spot assessment when they arrive at a traffic accident. They assumed, because of the mangled van, that they may be dealing with a fatality. I lay in the hospital bed that night drifting in and out of consciousness and thinking how lucky I was. Or was I? Had lady luck stepped in to save us that night, or, was it a more divine intervention? I strongly felt it to be the latter. I felt a strong sense of being saved for another purpose. I had no idea what.

I made a full, speedy recovery, as did my friend. It wasn't long before I was back behind the wheel and driving more respectfully.

When I was 30 years old I started working for one of the UK's largest holiday companies. I was a holiday host and enjoyed mixing with all the customers. I then moved on to being an assistant entertainments manager. This role included the recruitment of staff. It was to change my life forever. I received an application from a young man named Stuart. On paper, he was ideal: young, full of enthusiasm, and above all, a ballroom dance champion. In short, ideal for our aged guests who liked to trip the light fantastic each evening in our ballroom.

The day of the interview arrived. Stuart arrived on time and I stood up to greet him with a smile and a handshake. Now, some people will scoff at the idea of love at first sight but this was the case with us. As we shook hands we felt an unfamiliar energy pass between us. It was that moment when I thought, 'You know what, I'm going to be with you forever'.

One of the first things Stuart did was to give me a reading. He regaled me with tales of his psychic past and his plans for the future. The reading mentioned some details about my grandparents. I only ever knew one of my grandparents, my dad's mother. When I phoned home to check on the information, every aspect of what Stuart had told me was correct. I was pleased more than surprised, as I knew Stuart had a unique gift, one which I was very much wanting to experience myself. This experience bonded us even closer and we became a couple.

It was 1996, 31st October, Halloween. A little corny, I know, but this was the date that would be another changing point in my life. Stuart and I were based in the South East of England, in a well-known, if not somewhat run-down town, Margate. In its heyday, it was THE place to be as it was so close to London. Just 36 miles from Margate is Pluckley, thought to be one of the most haunted villages in England. It was the backdrop for the well-received English TV comedy drama, *The Darling Buds of May*.

We were both working on Halloween and didn't finish until gone midnight. Sue, another holiday host and friend of ours, offered to drive us to Pluckley in her car. It was going to be an adventure to a haunted location. Our cameras and camcorders were all fully charged and we were ready to investigate. As we got nearer to the village our excitement grew. We drove passed a sign welcoming us to Pluckley.

At this point the engine warning light on the dashboard came on, meaning there was a problem. The car was still working, so we continued to the centre of the village and parked up. We got out of the car and began walking down a lane. It was pitch black outside and we could barely see, but we soon came to an odd-looking gnarled tree. We could hear a strange moaning that seemed to be coming from the tree itself. We thought some late Halloween trick or treaters were playing games with us – but there was no one there.

We walked back up the lane and moved on to a graveyard. Stuart and Sue moved ahead while I remained a few paces behind. It was peaceful and still, almost like watching the TV with the sound off. I was taking care walking along the narrow path between the graves when I became aware of someone's chin resting on my left shoulder. I quickly turned to see who it was, but there was no one there.

I ran to tell Stuart, and we decided to cut short our visit to the graveyard. Something just didn't feel right. We returned to the car, and then decided to drive down the lane we had walked earlier to see the old tree again. We pulled up by the side of the tree. It was still making very strange noises, almost human-like.

Suddenly, the car lights went out. Sue screamed. We laughed, but our laughter was cut short when the engine abruptly failed. Sue turned the key in the ignition numerous times in hopes to get started again. Nothing happened, it was dead. We got our cameras and camcorder out to film the anomaly, but discovered their batteries were drained of all the energy they had.

It was well into the small hours of the morning by then, and Stuart became aware of very dark spirits surrounding the car. He began to say a prayer. Sue put her key in again and to our relief the engine started, but, we still had no lights. We slowly drove past the graveyard and along the country road. When we drove past a sign informing us that we were just about to leave Pluckley, all the lights in the car came back on. We got home safely with a lot to talk about.

The following morning Sue took her car back to the dealership where she had bought it the week before. It was a new car. On examination, the engineers could find nothing wrong with it and found Sue's tale a little hard to swallow. One odd thing was that the electronic date on her car dashboard had reverted to 1970, a feat that the engineers claimed was impossible. But, there it was for them to see. It was from this moment on that I began to take more notice of the spirit activity around me and to assist Stuart in his work as a medium.

A year or so later Stuart was booking a course with some friends at the world-renowned Arthur Findlay College of Spiritualism and psychic sciences. It was a week-long course in mediumship and psychic development, and at the last minute, I decided to attend. The first day we were split into groups and assigned our tutor for the week. To our excitement Mr. Glyn Edwards, the course creator, was ours. Glyn was one of the country's top leading mediums and tutors. I had never done anything like this before.

Our group consisted of 22 people. The first thing we had to do was to sit in a large circle. Glyn led us in a meditation. When we were done and ready to begin, Glyn pointed to me and told me to stand up and ask for a message from spirit for someone in the room. I was so nervous. Glyn was aware I was totally new to this level of engagement. 'Close your eyes and ask for spirit to come forward', he suggested.

I stood there, eyes tightly shut, wishing, hoping, praying that something would come. To my surprise my dog, who'd passed a few years before, was in my mind's eye, leading me up a narrow country lane. I began to vocalize what I was seeing. I was taken to a small country cottage with ivy around the door. There was an old tin bath in the yard and chickens running freely. The house was surrounded by a white picket fence which looked freshly painted. At one side of the property there was a large tree with yellow and brown leaves hanging from it. The wooden, white front door opened and a lady in her eighties came out waving. She had her grey-white hair in a bun and was wearing a green apron with fishes on, which was dusted in white flour. The house number was 47.

I suddenly stopped my description and wondered if I was correct. Was it just my acting improvisation skills kicking in through nerves? I opened my eyes and everyone was silent. Glyn then asked the group if anyone could take the vision I had described in such vivid detail. Everyone was silent.

'Oh well' I thought. As I sat down we could hear the gentle sobbing of an older man in the group. Glyn asked him if he could take the vision. The man confirmed that every detail I had seen was correct. It was his mother's home in Ireland. He was most impressed with the apron description and the white picket fence. His mother was very house proud and painted the fence once a month, whether it needed painting or not. I was relieved and somewhat surprised. Glyn said to me, 'Excellent work my boy, I knew you could do it'.

The rest of the week was a real influx of knowledge and ability for me. It seemed that a light switch had been turned on inside of me. At the end of the week, Glyn stood up in a hall full of students and proclaimed that I was the most fulfilled student of the course. He went on to say that I had the ability to become versed in my skills of mediumship. Why? Because I never questioned how it happened. I have found if you 'overthink' or if you try too hard, it can create manmade blocks. I still never question; I accept that I have this ability and cherish every moment of it. It's far cry from the Sunday school boy who drove the nun's crazy asking, 'Why? Why? Why?'

How to use this book

We hope you enjoyed some of the formative experiences that launched us on our paths. We'll share with you now in these pages our tips and techniques for successful mediumship development.

As we advised earlier, first read through the book thoroughly, taking time to familiarize yourself with its content. Every medium works differently and finds their own technique of how to work with spirit. You can use this book verbatim, or use it as a guide or framework. Whatever you decide, make sure it feels right for you. The more comfortable you are, the easier it will be for mediumistic development to unfold. We have used the contents, exercises and tools in this book personally in our communication with the other side for years and with very good results. We teach this material in classes and have helped produce some fine professional mediums, whilst enhancing the workings of seasoned professionals.

Manage your expectations of yourself and others

Keeping and managing your expectations to a realistic, grounded approach is paramount. We urge you to be excited at the prospect of communicating with the other side but also to stay grounded. It takes time and effort to develop, and one message here and there, whilst should be celebrated, doesn't necessarily mean that you are ready for a 90-minute platform demonstration of messages. You need to monitor your messages as you progress and ensure that you are getting lots of confirmation from your friends, family or acquaintances that you are accurate with the information you are imparting.

Others may suddenly see you as a demigod who can communicate with anyone in spirit and can summon spirits if they wish. It's important to understand that in mediumship that we do not summon spirits. If you are a magical practitioner this may be different, depending on your own personal practice. Mediums make contact with spirits for the purpose of communication. We ask, and those who wish to, or can, respond.

Always let your client or sitter know that you are in development and that this is a practice session. Always be honest. If you feel you are getting no link with spirit, then say so and don't try to force things to come, or your subconscious could then come up with nonsensical banter that produces inaccurate results.

Don't force it to happen

Relax and don't force the gift or experiences to happen. They will occur in good time naturally, so go with the flow. Sometimes things happen straight away, but more often they take time to unfold. There is no rush, so just take your time and let it happen.

There is something called 'the law of reversed effect': if you try too hard to do something, it causes the reverse effect and stops you from progressing any further. For example, have you ever lain in bed and you just can't get to sleep no matter how hard you try? Therein lies your problem – you're trying too hard. Instead, just relax, clear your mind and allow sleep to happen naturally. The same goes with mediumistic development.

Mind the three P's

The three P's are all important to every medium and psychic:

- **Patience**. As with any new or expanding skill, patience is paramount. You must dedicate yourself to learning and growing as a human and spiritual being, and to finding your truth. Take your time and enjoy every minute of the journey. Celebrate whatever milestone you find in your development. At times development may seem to stop or plateau. You find that if you try to run before you can walk, things may not go according to plan. If your development seems to hit a plateau, it may indicate you need to spend more time on certain skills before you progress onto another.

- **Practice**. Ensure that you can practice your gifts regularly. You can't expect to make an omelette without breaking eggs. The same applies here – you won't get greater results from little or no practice. We recommend that you sit at least once a week. We all lead busy lives nowadays, but you should make that effort and discipline yourself to work it in with your schedule. This also sends a clear message out to spirit that you are dedicated to becoming a conduit for spirit, and in turn they will help you ever more. The old saying, 'God helps those who help themselves,' fits nicely here. Help yourself and spirit will give you everything you need to become a good and accurate spirit communicator.

- **Perseverance**. It's important to persevere with your development. Some individuals, like Dean, open up quickly, like the flicking on of a light switch. Others open up gradually, and some have blockages to overcome. Whatever your progress, it is important to persevere.

  One of our clients was a lady who came to us for training seven years ago. She sat in circle, open to the possibilities and determined to become a medium. She had had experiences as a child which were conditioned out of her by her religious parents. She knew she had some blocks to overcome.

  She sat with us for more than nine months without getting anything from spirit. She became a bit disheartened and asked us if it was worth her continuing. We said yes, as we knew this was part of her destiny. When she came the following week, we knew something had changed. Stuart told her that the barriers that were hindering her development were dropping. She agreed, saying that she had felt a presence that was her guide with her all week.

  That night in circle, she started getting impressions and sensations. By the end of the night she had delivered three accurate messages to the circle members. She was in tears of joy, elated that her perseverance paid off. This is our advice to you, too. Never give up, for you never know what wonders are just around the corner.

Keep an eye on ego

Part of being human is that we all have an ego. That's great, but it's what you do with it that's important. Whilst you are developing, don't allow your ego to pop up with negatives, such as 'you're wrong' or 'you can't do it'. Ignore those criticisms and understand that it's is just the ego doubting and questioning. Plough forward and don't let the ego put you off. Likewise, don't allow critical and sceptical individuals to discourage you, either.

On the other side of the matter, don't let delusions of grandeur get the better of you. Keep grounded in your approach and don't become ego-driven for fame and glory. If fame happens as a by-product of being a good medium, so be it. Always work with honesty and integrity. Never exaggerate or lie about anything, as sooner or later the karmic 'tie of the lie' might come and bite you on the backside. Spirit is all-seeing and hearing. Spirits work best with those who are genuine and passionate in their approach to mediumship.

Ignore Hollywood stereotypes

Hollywood has a lot to answer for when it comes to the portrayal of the paranormal, supernatural, and mediums. We love a good scary film as much as the next person, but the reality of these films is often all too different. Don't fall for the negative stereotypes.

Take the Ouija board as an example. This is a tool which is marketed as a game in the USA. In the UK, the Ouija has never been seen as a game, but as a very serious tool for spirit communication. It seemed to go underground, so to speak, in the 1990s but soon surfaced again, more popular than ever.

We have yet to see a film that portrays it in good light. That doesn't sell tickets at the box office. It's a real shame the Ouija has acquired such an ominous reputation, as it is merely a tool for communicating with the other side. It is, in our opinion, neutral. In my practice as a child, it seemed like the board created my experiences, but that was not the case. Things were happening in my house long before the board came into play. The board allowed us to communicate with what was there, but didn't cause the phenomena. If the board is used with caution and spiritual protection, then you may see some lovely results. We have seen some very healing results of people using the board bringing comfort and closure and healing grief. We will have much more to say about the Ouija and similar spirit boards later on.

Except for a few films, ghosts and spirits also seem to have a negative slant put to them, which is rarely the case in real life. Some of

24

the 'haunted' properties we've investigated over the years are in fact cases of spirit visits from family members – nothing negative, just their loved ones checking in and saying hello, or the old inhabitants looking around what was once their home.

Mediums in film are often portrayed as eccentric, overly dramatic individuals. They have strange appearances and manners of dressing, and they act out when confronted by the (usually negative) spirit presences. They contort, scream, act as though they can't breathe, and claim to be attacked – in short, they do the 'floppy tuna' act.

In actuality, mediums are calm, focused, professional, and always in control.

Don't buy the Hollywood image of the paranormal, or what being a medium is all about. Understand that mediums are not expected to spontaneously become possessed or terrified. Learn first-hand through this book what the reality of mediumship is all about. We are on this journey of wonder and hope to see you down the path soon.

CHAPTER 2

THE ART OF MEDIUMSHIP

The art of spirit communication, or mediumship as it's more commonly known nowadays, has been around since the dawn of time. Millions of people around the world in all cultures and from all kinds of backgrounds have been encountering spirit and supernatural happenings. Ancient cave drawings seem to depict contact with other worldly beings, winged creatures with feathers (perhaps angels) and flying craft (perhaps UFOs). Clearly, we have been aware of other realities since our earliest days.

Our work and experiences have given us evidence and personal proof that we don't just 'die' and that's it. We have found that this has given us, and others, great comfort. We know that death is not the end, and you can also know that as truth, through developing your own mediumistic gifts. You can see first-hand the wondrous world of spirit communication. In our work, not a day goes by without someone contacting us for readings, spells, workshops or regaling us with their own stories of spirit communication.

One of the earliest documented accounts of the use of a medium is the 'Witch of Endor' in the Christian bible. The story tells about Saul, the king of Israel, who needs advice concerning a coming conflict with the Philistines. He consults prophets and dreams, but gets no answers. In that day, necromancy, or consulting the dead for advice, was a common practice, but earlier Saul had driven out all the necromancers in the land. Desperate, he disguises himself and visits the Witch of Endor, who claims she can summon the spirit of the dead prophet, Samuel. This she duly does for the king. Samuel delivers bad news. Saul's army will be defeated and Saul will die as well in battle the very next day. The prophecy comes true – Saul's forces are smashed, and in despair he commits suicide.

Direct spirit communication is important in many religions and spiritual traditions around the world. In truth, no one 'owns' spirit communication, and mediumship transcends religion and is available to all who seek.

Mediumship especially became important in Spiritualism, a religious movement that began in the USA in the nineteenth century and ignited a firestorm of interest. The match that lit the fire was the Fox family of Hydesville, New York, who had three daughters, Margaret, Kate and Leah. Apparently, they lived in a haunted house with a spirit that made noises. Margaret and Kate discovered that they could communicate with this entity by rapping back, and soon they were spelling out messages in a tedious method of rapping through the alphabet.

This novelty captured a lot of attention. The rapping phenomenon followed the girls wherever they went. The Fox sisters became mediums, giving public demonstrations of their ability to communicate with many spirits through rapping. Eventually the oldest daughter, Leah, joined the act as well.

Despite their success, the Fox sisters had a tumultuous career. They were, like most mediums that followed them, accused of fraud. One of the sisters even confessed to fraud, but then later recanted her confession. We'll let you make up your own mind on them. The

28

significance of the Fox sisters is that they played a key role in the establishment of Spiritualism. So many mediums sprang up in upper New York State alone that it became known as 'the burned over district'.

Spiritualism gained momentum on both sides of the Atlantic. It also became part of a social feminist movement. Women who became mediums could do outrageous things such as earn their own money and perform on stage. Mediumship provided some independence that women had not enjoyed – and they received public attention too.

There was no shortage of talented male mediums, and both men and women gained fame for their abilities to contact the dead. People flocked to see them. Scientists studied them in an effort to authenticate their results, and to seek proof of survival of death.

Interest in mediumship escalated into the early twentieth century. By the early 1920s, mediumship was all the rage. In the UK alone, it was estimated that there were more than a quarter of a million practicing Spiritualists, with thousands more running their own séances and spiritualist circles. Participants included all sorts of people in society, including royalty and figure heads.

Many people were attracted to séances because of the phenomena that were produced. Megaphones called trumpets were used to amplify disembodied spirit voices, and sometimes astonished sitters saw the trumpets float about the room. Some mediums were famous for producing apports, or objects that materialized out of thin air. Tables levitated, rapping sounded, and mysterious writing appeared on slates, allegedly by spirit hands. The most sensational feat was the production of ectoplasm, a filmy white substance that exuded from a medium, often through the mouth, that was used to form spirit faces, hands, and even complete body forms.

In every field, there are always unscrupulous individuals who attempt to defraud people, and Spiritualism was no different. Not surprisingly, some physical mediums such as the American Davenport brothers – who had training in stage magic – were exposed for using stage trickery during their séances. The Davenports were not the only ones. Unfortunately, truth and fiction became quite blurred. Mediums with genuine talent and ability sometimes resorted to tricks just to keep the hungry crowds satisfied.

Fraud disillusioned many researchers, and also many in the public. Physical mediumship waned in popularity, replaced by platform or gallery style mediumship, in which the medium is the messenger, delivering information from the dead to the living.

Over time, mental mediumship found its rightful place and is back in the hearts of the public. This style of mediumship is performed on television, on stage, in Spiritualist churches, and in countless private readings and circles, and is always popular. Simply put, there are not enough good mediums to go around to cope with the demand.

You could be one of the next mediums delivering messages from the world beyond!

What is mediumship?

Mediumship is a method of communicating with the spirits of those who have passed on into the world beyond. The 'place' we go to when we leave our mortal coil has many names depending on religious or agnostic beliefs and cultural backgrounds. Whether you call it heaven, the Summerland, the afterlife, the world beyond, the underworld, or the spirit world, human efforts to use mediumship to contact those residing there have gone on since time and the ages began. There has been a massive resurgence of interest in the past 30 years or so, due in part to an increase in popular interest in the paranormal, spirituality, alternate realities, and contact of all kinds.

Mediumship can be put into two categories:

Mental mediumship

Mental mediumship is the more common type of mediumship found today. Mental mediumship works through the mind of the medium.

Everything comes from and through the medium – there are no external physical phenomena. Mental mediumship can include clairvoyance, clairaudience, clairsentience and claircognizance, all skills we will address in this book.

Most mental mediums are aware of what they are receiving and giving. They may have one or more spirit guides who help filter the contacts and messages. In earlier times, these spirits were called 'controls', a term still used by some today. Contemporary spirit guides may also be the dead, angels, or higher beings of various names.

Mental mediumship involves entering a lighter or shifted state of consciousness that enables the flow of energy and messages from the spirit realm. For many, it's like entering a state of meditation. Some mediums go into trance, deeper states in which they may not be aware of what is being said through them. They may undergo physical changes, such as a marked change in voice and manner of speaking, postures and even transfigurations of the face.

Trance mediumship is often thought to be physical mediumship, but generally comes under mental mediumship, as it still involves spirit communicating through the mind of the medium. Some trance mediums, however, feel that spirit does a temporary physical takeover of their body in order to speak through them and demonstrate their characteristics. Trance is a bit of a grey area as some physical mediums (see below) also use trance in physical work.

If you go to a public demonstration or gallery style mediumship, the medium will often be fully alert and awake, often on their feet walking around and interacting with the audience whilst giving messages from communicating spirits. The medium is in a shifted state of consciousness, but is still able to be fully present with the audience.

Most mediums will meditate before giving a demonstration, getting into 'the zone' if you like. This is an important preparation, as it moves you away from the mundane world and gets you in the correct mindset where spirit can give you more detailed messages.

We have not included exercises on trance work as it's important to develop your other mental mediumship skills. Trance is an altogether different area of development.

Physical mediumship

Physical mediumship features physical acts and phenomena that can be witnessed by those present. A good physical medium usually, but not always, enters a deep trance state. We have seen good physical mediums produce physical effects while in a light trance, too. Physical phenomena include ectoplasm, apports, taps or raps about the room, voices, apparitions, spirit lights, odours, breezes, discarnate voices (voices coming from thin air) and transfiguration (a change in physical appearance). Very few mediums today produce ectoplasm, which is highly controversial.

If the medium is in a deep trance, then it may be possible for a spirit to communicate through them with the aid of the medium's guide or control. Other times in deep trance, the medium may just hold space and use their energy to help spirit manifest phenomena.

Physical effects take a huge amount of energy. Therefore, many of these types of demonstrations are done with several sitters in a séance. The combined energy of the group can be utilized to help such manifestations. It's important to note here that as a sitter or medium, your energy is not drained by spirit. The spirits are merely using the collective energy of the group.

Groups of people create energy without the participants even noticing it. Have you ever been in a room full of people only to notice you become very warm? What is heat but energy? The collective energy happens naturally. When a group of people concentrates on spirit contact and the desire to experience something, the collective thought and emotional energy create a thoughtform, which is like a battery that spirit can utilize. This is why thoughts of all kinds generated in daily life are so important. Think positive and you'll be positive.

A person contemplates on how best to develop mediumistic ability.

Frequently Asked Questions

What is the difference between mediumship and channelling?

This is one of the most frequently asked questions that has arisen in recent years as the term 'channelling' has become increasing popular. We've found that views differ somewhat in the UK and US. Some feel they are one and the same, whereas others feel that it is dependent upon who or what you are communicating with. Our descriptions are a consensus of the opinions of mediums and channellers, and based on our own many years of experience.

Mediumship is an ability to communicate with the spirit world. This is the means by which your loved ones, or ancestors who lived on this earth as mortal human beings, can establish a link to talk to the living.

Channelling is a form of communication that focuses on beings or entities that have not lived a mortal, human existence on earth. In channelling, you may be in contact with angels, faeries, galactic healers, and even extraterrestrials. Any kind of nonhuman entity can be channelled in much the same ways that mediums make contact with the dead, such as in light altered states of consciousness or deep trance.

The entities can deliver profound wisdom, and it is interesting to hear what they have to say. Popular examples of channelling are messages from the Pleiadians, the Arcturians, and individual messengers such as Kryon.

We will not go into channelling in this book, as our focus is on communicating with the spirit world.

What is the difference between mediumship and psychic ability?

Another popular question we hear is, 'Are mediumship and psychic ability the same thing'? When people want readings, sometimes they are unsure whether to see a psychic or medium, and some think they are the same thing. It depends on who you ask. There are differences, but also crossovers.

Let's try and move away from 'labels' here, as they can be very limiting. Mediumship and psychic ability are two different frequencies of energy, or different radio stations, if you will. The radio stations may be on different frequencies but sometimes they still play similar types of music. It is the medium or psychic who chooses which frequency to tune in to. Many times they do both, which has created the term 'psychic medium'.

Every medium and psychic has their own way of working. All mediums are psychic, for mediumistic ability is an advanced form of psychic ability. Mediums achieve a very finely tuned spiritual vibration, the result of which is being able to reach out to the spirit world with ease.

However, not all psychics are mediums. Whether through choice or circumstance, some psychics do not feel the need to communicate with the other side and to give spirit mediumship readings or platform demonstrations. Their psychic abilities may be used for reading the energy of a person or client to get impressions, thoughts, feelings and information about them to help guide the reading. They may work in all sorts of ways from remote viewing to healing. That said, many psychics work with human spirit guides, highly evolved spirits who lived a human existence on earth at one time. They are able to gain information from them, so, couldn't this also be seen as mediumship? We believe so! This shows that there can be cross over between psychic and mediumistic abilities.

A psychic works on a particular frequency of energy that is different from mediumship. They usually tune into your energy and can help you explore and understand your feelings on a holistic level. Some psychics may use divination tools to enhance the information. The most common tools are Tarot cards, angel and other kinds of oracle cards, runes and so on. A psychic reading can help you understand the past and present, and see possibilities about the future. The reading can also see other aspects of your life and help you to see it from many different angles. It's important to remember that you have free will and power over your own destiny. All psychics work in many different ways, and no one should ever be 'labelled' with one size fits all.

A reading with a medium is all about the evidence that spirit brings forth so that you will understand who is communicating from the other side. You may get names, places, descriptions and characteristics that are all relevant to the person who once lived. The details are usually followed by relevant messages for you.

So, you can now see the differences to consider when deciding what kind of reader you may want to visit. We are both psychics and mediums, meaning we work on both levels and can offer different types of readings depending on your needs.

When you book a reading with any professional, state what you are looking for, such as a message from someone who has died, or advice about your love life or career. Make sure you connect with the person who has the appropriate skills.

Psychics can expand to become mediums, and many do. Over the years we have run workshops specifically for psychics to elevate their abilities to communicate with spirit. The results have always been phenomenal. We must, of course, remember that we all have innate psychic and intuitive abilities whether finely tuned or still in the raw. Should you wish to develop these gifts further, all it takes is dedication and practice.

Why do some people have contact with the dead and some do not?

Why is it that some people are experiencers of spirit, even from an early age, and others seem to be devoid of any kind of encounters? We believe that everyone is born with at least some natural ability for psychic and mediumistic skill. There are many reasons why experiences are uneven.

Some people are brought up not to believe in psychic phenomena, the spirit world, ghosts and apparitions, alien beings, and the like. This type of conditioning can have a profound effect. It can repress natural ability and close a person off from many wonderful encounters in life, and not just paranormal ones. Such conditioning can continue into adulthood, especially if a person is persuaded that there is 'no scientific evidence' to support anything beyond the physical world.

These 'mind barriers' are hard to crack, but not impossible. If you have no desire to question and seek the truth, then those barriers may always remain. Even when these people experience something unexplainable, the blinkers are on and they come up with another reason behind it. Sometimes their 'rational explanation' is more ludicrous than the possibility of spirit contact. Similarly, people whose religious belief condemns this kind of work could also have mind barriers against experience.

Others who simply have no interest in the subject tend not to readily recognize spirits signs, either. Signs can come in many ways and sometimes are very subtle.

Coins randomly appearing, white feathers that show up when you are seeking an answer and butterflies out of season are all ways spirit can reach out to you. Be open-minded to the possibilities.

We have found over the time that a big group of non-experiencers are living in denial. It's incredible how many times that someone has said to us, 'I don't believe in all that stuff', only to go on to tell their own paranormal experiences in great detail, then clam up if you ask questions. Sometimes these sorts of experiences frighten people. We understand that. Mediumship and its practice for most is about communicating with spirits from the light, your loved ones, and the loved ones of others. So, you shouldn't have any scary experiences with mediumship.

However, there are times when unsettling experiences can occur with mischievous visiting spirits or earthbound spirits. Earthbounds are spirits who, for a variety of reasons, have not yet passed on but have remained in a twilight realm bound to earth. They can be lost, confused and even angry, especially if they are hanging on in order to settle some old score. Uncertainty over how to deal with these spirits may account for the reluctance of some individuals to talk about their experiences. They bury their heads in the sand and are happy to leave them there in fear of 'it' coming back. Sometimes this works with pesky or playful spirits and sometimes it doesn't.

It's not our job or anyone's to make people believe in the spirit world. We respect everyone's views and always feel it's a matter of each to his or her own. Whatever works for you is fine. We never preach, but we are happy to teach all who have a passion and openness for spirit work.

CHAPTER 3

LAYING THE FOUNDATION

W e now dive into practical exercises that will pave a smooth road for your mediumistic development. People often ask if doing these exercises will also increase psychic and intuitive abilities, as well as channelling and healing abilities. The answer is most certainly yes. The exercises in this book are specific to mediumship, but you will find that the skills are transferable to other areas of spiritual development.

Many of our mediumship students have reported a significant increase in psychic ability and prophetic dreams. Their Tarot and oracle card readings become more in-depth and insightful, and they experience a greater sense of feeling loved and protected. In time, you may feel these things too, but keep in mind your ultimate goal: communicating with spirit.

Mediumship and psychic development require good knowledge of the aura and energy centres known as the chakras. These wonderful fields of spiritual energy help us on so many levels whether we are conscious of it or not. Mediums, healers, psychics and others who work with such energies understand the importance of developing awareness of them and their functions. We will touch upon them from a mediumistic viewpoint.

The Aura

The word 'aura' comes from Greek and Latin influence to mean 'breeze' or 'wind' or 'breath'. In middle English, it means 'gentle breeze'. Whatever its origin, 'aura' is a term used by many psychics and energy practitioners to denote the field of energy that emanates from and surrounds the human body. The aura can be read psychically to gain insightful information about a person. The colours, size and fluctuations of the field all mean something relevant.

Auras change in shape and colour/s, depending upon the state of your mind, body and spirit. Someone who has been ill, for example, or is going through a stressful time, can have an aura that is faint in appearance with what looks like tears or holes in the field. The colours may appear darker and less vibrant, or foggy and murky. The aura reveals imbalances and even the early onset of disease.

Spiritual people and psychic practitioners of all kinds should develop a good, strong auric field. Some may show colours of blues and purples for healing and green for balance and attunement to nature. Others may have white, gold or silver in the aura, associated with being a highly evolved spiritual person with a strong connection to the divine. Every colour in the spectrum may show up in a person's aura. It's quite common to have more than one colour, all pointing to your lifestyle and path. It's important to note that the auric colours and densities continue to shift throughout the day. We've found that this happens as our energy levels, thoughts, feelings and emotions change. This is quite natural and underlines why keeping thoughts and feelings as positive as possible helps to maintain a strong aura.

The aura can be captured by certain kinds of photos or a type of photography called Kirlian, named after the man who discovered it. In 1939, a Russian scientist named Semyon Kirlian discovered that if an object on a photographic plate is subjected to high-voltage electricity, an image forms that appears to be an energy field around the object.

This process was adapted in the early 1990s to a type of photography popular at psychic fayres and events. The aura photograph is produced by a measurement of electromagnetic energy obtained through galvanic skin response. Your hand is connected to electric modules wired to a computer and camera, and an image is produced of a halo of colours around your head and shoulders.

At a psychic fayre, you usually get a printed handout with your photo explaining what your aura means at the time the photo was taken. Sometimes a psychic will give you a mini-reading decoding the auric photo with personal detail.

Galvanic skin response picks up fluctuations in emotions and energy levels, so if you return for another aura photo later in the day, for example, your aura may look quite different. Nonetheless, you can learn a lot about yourself and the strength of your energy field from aura photographs.

In regard to mediumship, the stronger your aura the stronger your connection to spirit. It's like a HDMI cable that connects your TV to a DVD player. You can get one for a small amount of money that will do the job but won't necessarily be the best quality signal. If, however, you invest more money in a cable with gold plated connections, you can physically see the difference with the high definition connection.

You don't want to just do the job though; you want to be a gold-plated medium, able to get the best possible connection. If you do your exercises in this book and follow the guidelines below for healthy habits, in time your aura will become strong, radiant and ready for the task at hand. As the subtle energies of spirit blend with your aura, you will get a strong link to spirit.

Keep the aura strong and vibrant

In your everyday life – going to work, shopping, banking, and so on – you can encounter all sorts of unwanted energies that can drain you and bring your own energy field down. There is a simple thing you can do on a daily basis to ward those energies off.

This technique is used by people the world over and is simple, yet very effective. Try it and see how you feel after even one day with this protection about you. Do it first thing after you have gotten ready for the day. It can be done in less than a minute, and if done daily, you will reap great benefits.

Exercise: Building A Protective Shell

Sit comfortably in a chair. Visualise a white light coming down from the universe. See its beam coming closer to your head and say, *White light,* divine, come my way, envelop and protect me throughout this day.

This gives the divine light permission to surround you. Notice its texture and how it feels. It may be like a warm waterfall, a big hug, or a big bubble. Whatever you feel is right for you. See yourself surrounded, head to toe, front to back, in this egg-shaped force field of positive energy, and know with confidence that it will deflect all unwanted and negative energy. Feel more energized and happy all round.

In the next chapter, we offer guidance for healthy lifestyle habits. If you follow those as well and combine them with these exercises, then your aura is sure to be vibrant.

The Chakras

Here we will talk about eight chakras from the viewpoint of mediumship and psychic development. We include the seven main chakras plus the ear chakras, which govern the ability to hear the voice of spirit.

The word 'chakra' is Sanskrit meaning 'wheel'. The chakras are vibrant, glowing circles of energy that penetrate the body and extend into the aura. They begin at the base of the spine and permeate the body from the back through to the front. The chakras each have specific shapes and colours, and they rotate clockwise as they process the vital life force from the universe. Each chakra governs specific body functions, and correlates to thoughts and feelings related to particular areas of life.

Below is an outline of each chakra and what part of life it influences. The chakras reflect the state of our physical, mental, emotional and spiritual health. When a healer, medium, or psychic looks at a person's chakras, they can see which are functioning well, and where there are weaknesses or trouble spots. Murky colours and sluggish speeds show where cleansing, healing and help are needed.

Each chakra should be kept cleansed and vibrant to the best of our abilities. The stronger the energy of each chakra, the stronger will be that area of your life. A common example that we see frequently are shadows or blockages in a chakra. Some people who have constant sore or groggy throat often have a throat chakra blockage. This may be because they feel they have been trying to talk to someone without success, or they want to stand up to a bully but are unable to do so. Some individuals have difficulty expressing who they are. These and other issues can cause an energy blockage around the throat energy centre. By clearing this blockage, the person is then able to speak their truth with confidence and conviction. Of course, if you have a sore or groggy throat always seek medical advice first as it may be caused by an ailment.

It is important from a mediumship perspective to have the chakras as open and vibrant as they can be, as the more 'energetically' open you are, the easier spirit can get their message across. If a spirit wishes to pass on details about an area of life that relates to a chakra that is not fully open or vibrant, then the details can be a little clouded. With openness comes clarity.

The functions and colours of chakras

Here are the eight chakras (including the ear chakras) in order from the root chakra (base of spine) to the crown chakra (top of head). We have concentrated on their mental and emotional associations.

1. **Root chakra – ruby red:** Located at the base of the spine, the root chakra is related to physical security such as career, finances, personal safety, home, material possessions, desires and needs.

2. **Sacral chakra – orange:** Located just below the navel above the root chakra, this centre relates to physical pleasures, sex, food, alcohol, exercise, weight, health and your appearance.

3. **Solar Plexus chakra – yellow**: This chakra is located above the navel and just below the rib cage. It serves as your personal power centre. It's not uncommon in mediumship that spirit will link to this centre, as it has great amounts energy that can help spirit to make communication clearer. Spirits do not drain the energy, but use it to amplify the signal, if you like. You may feel at times a quiver or flutter in this area during spirit work. This is quite natural. This chakra is about personal power and control.

4. **Heart chakra – light green**: This one is located in the centre of the chest. It is related to love, relationships, emotional attachments, forgiveness and lack of forgiveness. Most importantly in mediumship, the heart chakra relates to clairsentience, or clear feeling. The

clearer and stronger the heart energy centre is, the more pronounced the 'sensing' side of the spirit message will be.

5. **Throat chakra – sky blue**: This is located, yes, you've got it, in the throat area. It relates to speaking out and communication in all forms. Speaking the truth in a kind way, expressing yourself vocally and not bottling it up, will ensure a good, clear throat chakra.

6. **Ear chakras – warm violet**: There are two ear chakras, one located just above each ear. These are your psychic ears and the portals to clairaudience (clear hearing), which is the ability to hear the voice of spirit and your guides. People also hear the voices of angels and the divine. Believe in what spirit says to you and gain trust with spirit using this faculty.

7. **Third eye chakra – indigo**: This is located in the centre of your eyebrows and relates to spiritual sight and clairvoyance (clear seeing). Many 'see' this as a triangle with an oval shape inside. This is the psychic eye. With your intention, you can open and close it, as you will learn in exercises later. For psychics, the third eye chakra relates to seeing the past, present and future. For mediums, it relates to seeing spirits and other beings.

8. **Crown chakra – purple**: Located at the top of the head, this chakra is likened to a hatch or window that enables spiritual wisdom and truth to flow into you. It is where claircognizance (clear knowing) comes into play. You don't know *how* you know something, you just do. The crown chakra relates to the divine, God, Goddess, or however you perceive the source of all being. Spirituality and trust also are closely related to this energy centre.

Expanding the energy of the chakras

People often ask how long it takes to open the chakras before they can demonstrate mediumship. In truth, the chakras are always open – they cannot be closed or switched off, as we are living, spiritual beings. These energy centres are integral to our lives as spiritual practitioners. In mediumship development, we open them further and expand the power they hold.

Remember that chakras constantly spin like wheels in a clockwise direction. One way to open them further and build their power is to visualize them spinning at a much faster rate. The faster they spin, the higher your vibrational energy. Thus, spirit contact and psychic work becomes much easier. Think of it as creating a booster signal. If you see them moving faster, you'll get to your destination quicker.

Exercise: Linking the Chakras with White Light

Focus your attention just above the pelvis at the front of your body. This is the area of the root or base chakra and the place to start linking the white light.

Visualise the chakras running up the body like a string of beautifully coloured lights. The string of the lights is celestial white, a spiritual cord that links all the chakras together, creating very high vibrations. This white light automatically cleanses each chakra as it links them together. Feel your mediumistic and psychic power growing in strength.

This is a great exercise to do before any kind of mediumistic or psychic work and will help you to get the most out of your session. In time, you will be able to do this exercise with ease in less than a minute. No need to rush this though, for if it is done properly, it can become a very powerful tool.

This next exercise builds on the link and will help your chakras, and your ability, even more. You will learn how to raise your spiritual vibrations for mediumistic benefit, and then lower them again for functioning in daily life.

Exercise: Lifting Spiritual Vibrations

See your red root chakra spinning clockwise, going faster, then see a spur of white light coming from it as it moves to your orange sacral chakra.

See your orange sacral chakra spinning clockwise, going faster, then see the spur of white light link your orange sacral to your yellow solar plexus.

See your yellow solar plexus spinning clockwise, going faster, then see the spur of white light link to your heart chakra.

See your vibrant green heart chakra spinning clockwise, going faster, then see the spur of white light link to your throat chakra.

See your sky-blue throat chakra spinning clockwise, going faster, then see the spur of white light move in two directions, one left and one right to each ear chakra.

See your warm violet ear chakras that look like two wheels spinning clockwise in unison, going faster, then see the two spurs of white light move inwards towards your third eye.

See your indigo third eye inside its triangle. The triangle remains still, but your third eye is spinning clockwise, going faster. Open the third eye wide, then see the spur of light linking to the crown chakra.

See your purple crown chakra, spinning, going faster, then see the spur of white light from the third eye link to your crown with the intention to open it wide. See the white spur of light shoot out the top of the crown and into the ether, ready to receive spirit communication.

Allow yourself to fully absorb all the energy from the chakras. Stay in the moment and enjoy the sensations. When the moment feels right, ready yourself for the return, slowing the chakras back to their daily life speed.

See the spur of white light coming down from the ether, into the crown. See your purple crown chakra, spinning, slowing down.

See the white spur of light move down to your third eye. See your indigo third eye spinning, inside the still triangle, slowing down. Note: The third eye is still all-seeing but in a more rested state.

See the spur of light journey to the left and right ear chakras. See your warm violet ear chakras spinning like two wheels, slowing down.

See the two spurs of white light move inwards towards your throat chakra. See your sky-blue throat chakra spinning, slowing down.

See the spur of white light move down to the heart chakra. See your vibrant green heart chakra spinning, slowing down.

See the spur of white light link to your solar plexus chakra. See your yellow solar plexus spinning, slowing down.

See the spur of white light link to your sacral chakra. See your orange sacral chakra spinning, slowing down.

See the spur of white light link your root chakra. See your red root chakra spinning, slowing down.

See a spur of white light moving down the legs and into the ground, anchoring your energy to the earth. Feel grounded, refreshed and energized.

After you have finished this exercise, relax and enjoy the sensation. You should be feeling energised yet peaceful and calm. Drink a little fresh water and make any notes about your experiences. Creating a record will enable you to look back on your journey with this exercise and track your progress.

Do this exercise often to keep the chakras cleansed and strong. It will also strengthen your spiritual power and in turn strengthen your connection to the spirit world.

Chapter 4

Opening and Closing to the Spirit World

In this chapter, we will build on what we have learned. If you have practiced the exercises given so far, you will have developed and refined your chakra energy centres and your spiritual vibration level. Now, let's practice opening and closing to spirit communication.

Opening

Correctly opening yourself and your energy centres initiates connection and lets spirit know that you are ready to receive. It also ensures you are in total control of the situation. Mediums who have been working for many years often do this automatically, ourselves included. We just have to say 'ready' and it happens. It's like flicking a light switch. As you develop on your path, you find how to create your own switch or trigger. It doesn't mean that you skip bits or create a deliberate shortcut, but it happens naturally as you become more aware of how your energy works for you.

The following exercise is a shorter version of the training exercises in Chapter 3, and is intended to accomplish the opening connection quickly. Notice how you feel and how your body responds, for you will get your own trademark signals to let you know when you are ready. For example, when I (Stuart) open, I feel a tingle through my body like running water – it's like, on your marks, get set, go! Then I'm off on my messages.

Exercise: Opening

Start with a prayer, affirmation, or incantation that is appropriate for your spiritual beliefs and prepares you psychologically and psychically to become a vessel for spirit. For example:

Mother and father God, please allow me to see, hear and feel your presence and what I need to know...

Great Spirit, let me be your voice on earth now...

I am now ready to receive from the spirit world...

Close your eyes and pay attention to your breath. With each intake breath feel yourself becoming lighter.

Visualize a purple energy at your base or root chakra, located just above the pelvis. See and feel that energy moving up the body with each breath. The higher it gets, the higher your vibration. Feel yourself almost shiver as your energy lifts. Keep going until you see the purple energy shoot out above your head and beyond. It looks like a cone coming out of the root chakra. This sends out a clear message that you are ready to receive messages. Your entire body tingles with high vibrational energy.

Closing and Grounding

Closing and grounding after every session with spirit allows you to come back to your 'normal state' and lets spirit know that you are finished communicating. If you stay in an expanded state, your energy will soon run low. Just as we need to cool down after a workout or exercise, we need to do the same in working with spirit. When you have finished a telephone call with someone, to stop it you hang up, or the line remains open and the telephone stops working. So, do a closing and grounding without fail.

The following exercise will help you anchor your energy and feel 'down to earth' once again, so to speak.

Exercise: Closing

Close your eyes and thank the spirit world and guides who helped you.

Take three deeps breaths in through your nose and out through your mouth, and then find your own comfortable level of breathing.

Visualize yourself with roots, like the roots of a tree, coming out of the bottoms of your feet and planting themselves into the earth. Feel your energy becoming more grounded and let the energy of Mother Earth anchor you to her.

This is a tried and tested exercise that is used by many psychics and healing practitioners. It is quick and simple, and gets results.

Eating and drinking something after meditation and spirit communication helps with the grounding process.

Now have a little snack and a drink. This will further help you feel grounded. You use a lot of energy in mediumship, more than you realise, so you are likely to feel a little peckish. Enjoy.

In all your sessions, spiritually warm up with an opening and cool down with a closing and grounding.

Frequently Asked Questions

Do mediums see, hear, or feel spirit all the time?

We are asked this question constantly, and the quick answer is no. In our early days, we were fortunate enough to be guided by some the best mediums around. They said to us that if we left ourselves open to receiving messages from spirit all the time we would soon burn out. This is so true, as we noted above.

Countless spirits are out there wanting to connect with someone here on earth. If we mediums left our channels open all the time, we would never be able to sleep or go anywhere without being asked by spirit to pass on a message. There is a time and place for everything, and spirit communication is no different.

When you work as a medium or spiritual practitioner, always remember that you have a life on earth too. Keep your relationships with family and friends as harmonious as possible. Ensure that you go about your everyday life and enjoy every minute. Keep all your activities positive. If there are any that aren't, replace them quick smart.

If there is an urgent message that we need to know about, such as Stuart's car episode in Chapter 1, spirit always know they can come through instantly. This doesn't happen often, but when it does, their insight has proved invaluable.

How should messages be handled?

One of the most invaluable pieces of advice we have been given over the years by many of our teachers is to not edit anything we receive from the spirit world. Everything received during a reading or demonstration, whether it be seeing something, getting a feeling, hearing something, or getting a general knowing, should be relayed to the sitter. Everything you experience happens for a reason, which may not be readily apparent to you, but will make sense to the sitter.

We gave a reading once to a lady at a Spiritualist church. The message came from her son who had taken his own life. He presented himself as a happy lad and the messages that came through were very uplifting to his mum. As we went on I (Stuart) became aware of a character called Zebedee from a children's television show called *Magic Roundabout*. This character had a big moustache and was mounted on a spring, which is how he got about. I saw the image of Zebedee bouncing on the top of a tin of baked beans. I had never seen that in the show, of course, but I could not immediately understand the meaning of what I was seeing.

I had a 'knowingness' that I should just say what I saw, so I did. I felt silly saying it, as it was the oddest of messages, or so I thought. I said to the woman, 'I'm getting a message that might sound odd, but feel I need to say it'. She listened with excitement as did her two sisters sitting either side of her. I described the image and without a pause, everyone present burst out laughing, looking at each other with such knowing laughter.

I said, 'You understand what I've said'?

The woman's response was, 'That's bang on, I know exactly what that means'.

The message meant something quite profound to them and it was excellent evidence. The woman did not elaborate, and to this day I don't know what that message meant. This experience taught me to always give off what I see, no matter how strange it may seem.

Remember, the message isn't for you as the medium, so you don't need to understand it. I did my job by giving it off and that's all that matters. Your clients and sitters are not under obligation to explain the significance of any message. The content may be highly personal to them. It's only important that they understand.

The reason I bring this up is that mediums, especially ones with little or no experience, naturally go through a doubting phase. You may think, 'That's not right' or, 'No it can't be' or 'Is my mind making this up'? Messages are given for a reason. Trusting them builds trust with spirit.

I went through this myself in my early days as a medium. I have since learned that everything you get during a demonstration or reading is relevant to the spirit communicating with you, and helps to validate the message for the person receiving it. Dean is amazing – he has always believed, accepted and trusted everything he has been given from spirit. He has always given everything off from the start and has given the most incredible messages.

What should I do if a sitter says they do not understand a message or that it is wrong?

Some mediums worry about hearing the word 'no' during a demonstration or a reading. They love the yes's as their clients are understanding the messages being given. However, on occasion you do have people say, 'No, I don't understand'. In response, some mediums (especially beginners) freeze and shut down their mediumistic side as self-doubt creeps in and the ego says, 'I told you can't do it'.

That is nonsense. Of course, you can do it! When a medium hears a 'no' from a sitter, it's something you should feel excited about. It usually means the message has a deeper meaning than the surface level.

First, ensure you are giving off exactly what you see, feel, hear or know. Ensure you are not editing it, or trying to make it fit in with what you think the message should mean. Remember the message is not for you, it's for them, or someone they may be connected with in the mortal world.

Ask the communicating spirit to clarify what they mean. Usually, you will receive additional information that you can give off which makes sense to the sitter. If, however, you still get an emphatic no, then suggest that they speak to a family member who would have known the deceased person and tell them of the message. Impress upon them that they do this to clarify the message, because spirit has given it for a reason.

Sitters will not necessarily know everything about a person in spirit. In fact, they may not know much at all, especially if, say, a relative died before they were born. We have been asked on a couple of occasions to give a missing piece to a family-tree. The spirits concerned were happy to oblige.

We once met a sceptic – we always say we only meet a sceptic once, as usually after a reading or demonstration they become believers or at least more open-minded. This particular man, whom we met thorough a social circle, was very closed off and said he didn't believe in the spirit world and mediumship. He wasn't being rude, but just was expressing his own take on things. We always respect people's beliefs.

We explained to him that he had two spirits with him. He laughed and said, 'Well, come on, then'. We went to a quiet room and began an impromptu reading, which generally we never do.

We connected with his grandmother. He understood everything we told him except for one thing: her name. We said her name was Anne, and he said, 'No'. We repeated that her name was indeed Anne. He said, 'You're spot on with everything else but her name is wrong, her name was Emily'. We gently insisted that Emily was not right and he should check it out. He said, 'I'm going to call my mum' and did so whilst we sat there.

'Mum' he said, 'you know Nanny Emily? Well, I've just had mediums give me a message from her. I relate to everything they said, but they said her name was Anne'.

There was a slight pause and he looked at us with his jaw dropped. 'Okay Mum, thanks', he said and hung up.

We knew the name Anne was right. We said to him, 'What did your mum say, then'? He replied that there were two Anne's in the family, which caused confusion, so his grandmother decided to use her middle name, Emily, as her first name to stop confusion. He was totally unaware of this and was blown away by this revelation. We are pleased to say that he is now a believer and a client.

Remember, it's not your job or anyone else's to make people into believers, but when the right situation presents itself, you may receive a sign from the divine that will help a person on their path in some way. You find yourself playing a role in something that is 'written' or meant to be.

So, trust, do not edit, and dig deeper if need be. Do not be afraid to hear the word no – you might be on the tip of a profound message.

Chapter 5

Enhancing Mediumship

When you embark on the spiritual path and wish to enhance your mediumistic and psychic ability, you may feel drawn to cleanse your mind and body of toxins, pollutants, chemicals, junk foods, alcohol and so on. In the development of mediumship and psychic abilities the following enhancements can help sharpen your skills. Cleansing the mind, body and spirit should always be high on the agenda. We are not here to preach, only to teach and share with you the steps we took ourselves to enhance our mediumistic and psychic abilities. Many of our students have adopted a similar lifestyle and have found a huge benefit in all areas. We describe why each of these 'enhances your chances' of making your spirit contact more detailed and profound.

Food and drink

We love our food, sometimes a little too much, but we recognize what sorts of foods resonate at a higher vibration than others. Some of the following are common sense measures for overall health, and many of them have positive effects on our spiritual health. Always consult a medical professional before making any changes to your diet.

Before we communicate with spirit, we always ensure that we have not eaten for at least 30 minutes after a meal or snack. When you are communicating with spirit you should feel as comfortable as possible. If your digestive system is working hard on the meal you have just eaten, then the body will have less energy to aid your spirit work. The type of meal to eat 30 minutes or so before spirit work is something healthy and light. If you have a huge pot roast with all the trimmings, despite it being yummy, it will sit heavily with you. Meat (particularly red meat) takes ages to digest.

Fresh vegetables, fruits, grains, salads and homemade soups are excellent choices. They are considered life force food and not only feed your physical body, but also nourish the spiritual body and its energy centres. Life force foods are 'natural', in that they have not gone through lots of processing with lots of additives and preservatives. Some people choose to eat organic produce, but this is down to your own choice. Some of us also have special dietary requirements. We all have common sense and know what we need to function. We just provide a little guidance from a mediumship development viewpoint.

Does being vegetarian make you a better medium or psychic? This is a question that comes up all the time. This is a deeply personal choice and one which you can make for yourself. We have both been vegetarians and meat eaters. At the time of writing of this book, Stuart is a vegetarian and Dean is a flexitarian, meaning he eats veggie foods 90 percent of the time and only chicken and fish on occasions. This has to do with Dean being a very fussy eater too! Overall, we eat a variety of foods that work well for us and ensure a balanced and healthy diet.

Some practitioners say 'yes,' a vegetarian diet benefits mediumship performance, and others say 'no'. It all comes down to personal choice and experience. I (Stuart) have found that being a vegetarian has sharpened my clairvoyance, claircognizance, clairsentience and clairaudience. Perhaps some of it has to do with the fact that I am very content in this way of eating. You can experiment with vegetarianism or not, and see how it works for you.

A healthy diet does make a difference overall, and there are many ways you can improve your diet. By having a healthier body, you will have more vitality and energy for working with spirit.

Drink-wise, it's a good idea to drink plenty of water every day, as this is a good conductor of energy. Alcohol is best avoided when you are working with spirit, because you want your experiences to be your own and not created by the alcohol. We do not drink any alcohol at all. In England, this is called 'tea-totalled', as we British are known for our love of a good cup of tea. It's just our personal choice and preference. We are not suggesting you give up alcohol, but, for spirit work we have found it's best to keep a clear head.

Physical exercise

It's good to make exercise part of daily life, if you can. You can exercise any way you want: a walk around the block, a jog in the park, a workout at the gym, taking the stairs instead of the elevator, washing your own car or someone else's instead of going to the car wash, and walking somewhere instead of driving. We all know what may work for us, but as with any change in the way you exercise, always seek advice form a medical professional first.

Exercise plays an important part in development. It's a proven fact that exercise reduces stress with the release of the feel-good hormones, 'endorphins'. These miracle hormones make you feel more relaxed, stress-free, calm, energised, confidant and focused – all the things you need for successful mediumistic unfoldment.

Cleansing

As the saying goes, 'cleanliness is next to godliness'. Showering and bathing are part of our unfoldment process, believe it or not. In the past, before sacred initiations and communing with spirits of the dead were undertaken, our ancestors ritually cleansed themselves, such as bathing in milk and honey or dipping into a sacred river. They did this to not only rid themselves of bodily grime, but also because they knew that communication with the spirits and the gods was special and sacred, and required cleanliness on all levels.

As it was back then, it still is now. You would not go out to a special evening at a restaurant, on a date, or to a party without showering or bathing, because you want to feel and look your best for that special occasion. Spirit contact is a special occasion and should always be looked on in that way.

Bathing and showering also bring a sense of well-being and relaxation. The more relaxed you are, the more the messages will flow. To your bath you can add all sorts of delicious smelling bubbles and fizzy bath balls, but make sure they are made of natural ingredients and are not full of chemicals. Using the best pure essential oils under the guidance of a qualified aromatherapist can be wonderful. Lavender and chamomile oils aid relaxation and ready you for meditation or sleep.

Another good cleanser to add to your bath, which is inexpensive and readily available everywhere, is sea salt. Not processed table salt, but natural, coarse sea salt. You can add a handful to the running bath water, giving it time to dissolve. Salt has always been a natural ingredient used by healers, mediums, and others who do spiritual work. It has potent cleansing properties for the mind, body and spirit, and helps to remove negative energy.

Ensure as you soak in the bath that your solar plexus and heart chakra are immersed below the water line if possible; if not then swish the water over those chakras. This cleanses away negative emotions that do not serve your highest good. Once you have soaked for a little while you can get out and let the water drain away along with unwanted thoughts or energies, leaving you feeling vital and ready for the task at hand.

For those of you who use a shower as opposed to a bath, you can have a wonderful spiritual cleansing shower. For the essential oils, put a couple of drops in an oil burner in the bathroom 10 minutes before the shower, which will give you the beautiful fragrance and vibrational essence of the oils. Sprinkle the sea salt onto the floor of the shower. To reduce its coarseness, which will be kinder on your feet, first grind the salt a little in a mortar and pestle or grinding mill. Alternatively, put the coarse salt in a baggie and use a rolling pin, to produce finer grains. Always ensure the surface is not slippery and use a shower mat for safety.

Once you get into the shower, let the water cascade down your body and let go of any thoughts that do not serve you. Swish your feet in the salty water, for thoughts and unwanted energies can be effectively removed through the feet. This is one of the principles of reflexology, an ancient and effective healing modality in which the energy meridians in the feet are massaged for overall physical effect.

These cleansing techniques will indeed help you in all areas of your life. Even if you are not due to communicate with spirit that day, still use the techniques. It's all about looking after not only your physical body, but also your spirit body, the aura, and the chakras. These practices will strengthen you and your energy centres and allow for a happier existence all round.

Negativity diet

A negativity diet has nothing to do with food! During your development and in life in general, it's a good idea to keep negative situations and unnecessary drama at arm's length.

Some people can be negative and overly dramatic without being aware of their attitudes and behaviour. They may be very closed-minded and cynical, not just concerning mediums, but in other areas of their life too. People who constantly gossip and judge others and try to get you involved in their negative thinking can be quite draining. It's not unusual on the spiritual path to find that you make new friends along the way, and the negative ones you once knew gravitate to others who share their negative approach to life.

Keep your own thoughts in check. Be as positive as you can. Life can sometimes throw difficult things to us all at one time or another. It is all about how you approach things. A positive mental attitude can work wonders. Try not to sink into the victim mentality, for it's hard to get out of! Strive to be the best person you can be and your development can start to unfold further.

Sacred jewellery: to wear or not to wear

Sacred jewellery has been worn through the ages and is even more popular today, with many beautiful choices available. Does it make a difference in your spiritual work what you wear? Our students often ask us if they should wear a symbol of their belief system, or a certain a gem stone, such as amethyst, or some sort of magical charm with sacred herbs. We both wear sacred jewellery in our work because it is part of our expression of who we are, and we feel an affinity with our pieces. But do they make a difference in spirit communication?

We were intrigued by this question, as we had heard different things from our different teachers throughout the years. We have been trained by Spiritualist mediums, psychics, magical practitioners, and others. Many say 'yes' and some say 'no'. This is what we discovered ourselves. At no point are we telling you whether you should wear something or not; rather, it's a personal choice.

Some of our past teachers recommended wearing gemstones, saying that the vibration of the stones lifts your vibration from earth's dense energy, thus making spirit communication easier. In contrast, others stated that if you wear such jewellery it will lift your energy to a level that will be inaccessible to spirit and will only be appropriate for reaching angels and ascended masters.

We took both schools of thought with respect but needed to see what worked for us. We did various reading and demonstrations with and without sacred jewellery of all kinds, and we discovered that for us personally, it made no difference to the quality of the communication. We were happy with that discovery and for us it comes down to personal choice. I, Stuart, wear jewellery most of the time, whereas Dean will wear one piece on occasions, or if he feels drawn to it. Make a choice you are happy with and wear it with pride.

Symbols for protection

Some people new to the path wonder if it is essential to wear a symbol of some sort for their protection during spirit work. Remember not to get in the mind-set of Hollywood that holds that if you commune with the dead, someone will attach to you and haunt you in a negative way. This is extremely rare. If you keep your aura heathy and start out right with prayers or affirmations for protection, you are sure to have a safe and effective time, and will feel uplifted and in awe of the whole experience.

Sacred symbols are worn by many people based on their spiritual belief systems. Some wear conspicuous jewellery so everyone can see it, and others are subtle. This, again, is down to personal choice, and whatever works for you is the best way. Always be yourself and be proud of who and what you are. Many people feel that a symbol of their spiritual or religious belief is automatically an amulet, or protection against dark energy and forces. A Christian spiritualist, for example, might wear a crucifix, and a witch might wear a pentacle.

An amulet is any object that is magically or psychically charged to keep away negativity. A talisman, by comparison, is charged to bring something to the wearer, whether it be wealth, happiness, love, and so on. The easiest way to remember this is amulet, A= away and talisman, T= Towards.

I always wear my pentacle as an amulet. It makes me feel complete, but that's me. If you don't feel an affinity with any symbol you can use a gem stone as an amulet instead. Gems and stones each have their vibrational properties, and you can select accordingly.

If you have no wish to wear a symbol, perhaps you are agnostic in your approach or perhaps even a little sceptical. That's all good, too. You could use a crystal or stone for protective purposes. For example, smoky quartz, amethyst, tourmaline, hematite, and moonstone are renowned for their protective properties. They have a great history and we've found them to be invaluable.

You can purchase crystals and stones as jewellery or simply get a tumbled stone and put it in your pocket or carry it in a purse.

CHAPTER 6

DEVELOPING THE CLAIRS

In mediumistic work, we use the extended abilities of our physical senses. They are called the 'clairs' because the psychic component of each sense has a name based on the French word 'clair' for 'clear'. All our physical senses, plus our ability to 'know' and 'sense' something, have their extended psychic components. Here we will focus on the 'fab four' clairs most commonly used in mediumship: seeing, hearing, sensing and knowing.

Clairvoyance

Clairvoyance comes from the French word meaning 'clear seeing'. Mediums use this ability to see spirit clearly and the images the spirit wishes to show them. Clairvoyance may be subjective, that is, it does not register in your physical sight, but in your mind's eye or third eye – images appear in your mind. Objective clairvoyance manifests as if you are seeing spirit in the same manner as you would physically see a person standing in front of you. There is a fine line between the two, as you are still using your 'clairvoyant ability'.

We have both experienced objective and subjective clairvoyance. Both give good evidence. The rule of thumb is, just go with it. If what you see can be verified by your sitter or client, that is what counts.

Clairvoyance enables a medium to give detail and depth to a reading. For example, you can describe exact physical appearances, such hair colour and style, stature, skin tone, fashion sense, and even moles, birthmarks and tattoos. We have both seen such details over the years, and they have given our sitters solid evidence of who they are in touch with.

Clairsentience

Clairsentience comes from the French word meaning 'clear sensing'. Clairsentience enables a medium to experience what the spirit person felt on earth, such as their emotional state, personality, physical conditions they had, or perhaps symptoms and conditions concerning how they passed away. You may literally feel their joint pains, back aches, migraines and arthritis, to name a few. Don't worry though, these feelings don't stay with you after you are done. There are so many ways clairsentience can help you feel and sense what the communicating spirit wants you to know.

I (Stuart) gave a reading once when someone's mum came through. The spirit lady said, 'They didn't believe me' and started showing me all the pains she suffered. She was referring to the doctors and their lack of compassion to her plight. Although this was sad for her children to hear, the sceptical son was blown away by the evidence and admitted later he is a better person for opening his mind.

Clairsentience is related to the heart chakra in particular, and it is easy to develop it further. Notice we say, 'develop it further', for everyone has clairsentient abilities from the start. Perhaps you haven't realized it.

Ask yourself these questions:

- Have you ever walked into a room after someone has had a heated disagreement? You could cut the atmosphere with a knife? You have 'clear sensed' the energy.

- Have you ever seen someone you don't know, and even though they show no physical signs, you 'feel their pain' whether physically or emotionally? You have clear sensed the energy.

- Have you ever met someone for the first time, and they seem nice but you can't put your finger on why you don't like them, only to find out later you were right? Yes, you sensed the energy.

If you answered yes to one or more examples above, it should prove to you that you are indeed clairsentient. Notice that we used the term 'sensed the energy'. Keep in mind that spirit is also energy and can be tuned into, or sensed, fairly easily. That's what clairsentience is all about.

One of the easiest ways to develop clairsentience is to use a technique called 'psychometry'. Some of you may have seen this done before by a psychic or medium. Psychometry, sometimes called 'psychic touch', involves holding an object and receiving information and impressions from it. Objects retain energy from their owners and also from their uses. For example, if you hold someone's ring or watch, you can sense information about them, their emotions, and their lives. Even archaeological artifacts can be psychometrised.

Objects do not have to be old; however, the longer an object has been owned and used by a person, the stronger will be the energy imprints that it absorbs. If you try to psychometrise a new ring or watch, you will get few impressions from them, except, perhaps from the manufacturing process or the people handling them before they were acquired by the owner.

If an object has been owned by more than one person, impressions can be mixed and muddied. So, estate pieces, inherited objects and the like are not good candidates for mediumistic psychometry. The best candidates are personal objects that are worn frequently, such as jewellery, watches and clothing, followed by any kind of personal or household possessions, especially if they have had emotional significance to the owner. We have seen vases, cars, grandfather clocks and the very fabric of a building itself being touched for psychic impressions.

Metals are the best retainers of energy. Even car keys or home keys can work, for people are emotionally attached to their vehicles and homes. Clothing, because it is worn next to the body, will often have strong imprints. Stone, pottery and wood items are good. Even manmade materials can yield something.

Any object that has been handmade or assembled by the owner is an excellent candidate, regardless of material. The process of making or even decorating an object involves a person imbuing their energy into the object itself. Whenever you are attracted to an artist's work, for example, you are probably psychometrising the energy of the artist.
In the exercises section, we have included a psychometry exercise for developing clairsentience.

Clairaudience

Clairaudience comes from the French word for 'clear hearing'. Mediums use clairaudience to 'hear' what spirits have to say. It may just be a few words or a clear sentence. You may be able to detect accents or voice inflection or even mannerisms of speaking. We have heard people burp and make the odd fart here and there. Jokes aside, when this evidence has been mentioned to sitters, they have always validated it as something that person would always do in life.

I (Stuart) once did a reading at the Arthur Findlay College in London while I was attending a course in 2004. I was partnered up with a man from Denmark. He spoke good English, whereas I knew no Danish. I wondered how the communication would fare, and soon learned that language was no barrier. I began to describe the spirit I could see, which he validated. I then heard words from the spirit, words I did not understand or had never heard before. I explained this to him and he asked me to repeat them, so I did verbatim. He burst into tears and stood up and hugged me tightly. It was a very emotional reading.

The sitter then explained that his father, who was talking to me from spirit, had said, 'I am home and safe' in Danish. He went on to tell me that his father's last few words before he died were, 'I'm going home, I'll be safe'. This blew me away, and my experience will be treasured forever.

Claircognizance

Claircognizance is a lesser clair that is overlooked at times, but is very important in mediumistic work. Claircognizance means 'clear knowing'. Have you ever thought of something, or said something, and you thought, 'How on earth do I know that?' Well, that is claircognizance. You don't know how or why you know something, you just do. Sometimes words, visions and sensing are not needed, you just know what spirit wants to say or what their message holds. A 'knowing' comes over you. Accept that this happens and learn to trust what you 'know' to be true.

Exercises to Develop the Fab Four Clairs

Many of our students over the years have asked us which gift they should develop first – is one clair more important than the others? The short answer is that they are all equally important, as each clair can provide that all-important evidence that clients expect. You never know what small piece of information or impression will have a big impact on the sitter.

It is true that most mediums, certainly all the wonderful mediums we have met and worked with over the years, say that they have a dominant clair that they use more than the others. Sometimes the clair you use depends on the person in spirit.

As I mentioned above, clairaudience was the dominant clair with the Danish father. In other cases, it's clairvoyance, where I see spirits and can describe clearly what they are wearing, their facial features, physical disabilities, and even moles and birthmarks.

Overall, clairsentience is the most common clair that all mediums work with. It gives us the ability to feel as the spirit would have felt in their physical life. When we ask them how they passed from this world, they may be able to show us what they felt. I have often felt heart pain, stomach pains, blows to the head, strokes and other ailments that they may have had during life or which may have caused their passing. I have felt their emotional state, such as whether someone was always happy and having a good laugh. I have also felt spirits who have had severe depression and anxiety.

Using a combination of the four primary clairs can bring through wonderful evidence and make the reading a more in-depth and meaningful experience.

Below we have exercises for you to develop the four main clairs. Once you have begun this unfoldment you will find that the other, lesser-used clairs may begin to happen quite naturally. For example, clairgustance (clear tasting) can reveal foods that the spirit person liked and clairolfaction (clear smelling) can reveal perfumes and scents or cigarette and pipe smoke that may be associated with the communicating spirit.

These exercises are best done once or twice week to aid your development. They can be done as standalone exercises lasting 15 minutes each or they can be combined as you wish. For example: On Monday, you might choose to do two of the exercises, clairvoyance and clairsentience. This would last approximately 30 minutes. On Wednesday, you might choose to practice only claircognizance lasting 15 minutes. Then on Saturday you have time to practice all four exercises, which would take about an hour, and so on. The times for each exercise or for combining them is just a guide. Find your own comfortable pace at which to go. You may feel more drawn to develop a particular clair at certain times. That's fine, just go with the flow.

Please note, the exercises are best done in a sitting position. If you lie down you may find yourself falling asleep and will lose the benefit of the exercise. You may want to set a timer so that you are not thinking about keeping track of time.

Our advice to beginners is to take the process slowly and don't run before you can walk. Work on each clair individually and combine the exercises when you feel ready to do so. For those who have sat in circle or used other development exercises, you can go straight to combining exercises if you wish. Work at your own pace and decide for yourself what exercise/s you may wish to work on. You are always in control of your development.

Exercise: Developing Clairvoyance

Sit in a comfortable position. Close your eyes and breathe deeply in through the nose and out through the mouth. Allow yourself to relax and let go of any earthly thoughts or stresses. If your thoughts wander, gently return to focusing on the breath.

Bring your attention to the centre of your forehead, between the eyebrows. Feel that area becoming more energetic and active. Visualize a triangle between your eyebrows, and inside the triangle see an oval shape that is indigo in colour. This is your third eye, your centre of clairvoyance and spiritual visions.

Your third eye is ready to open. Tell yourself it is safe for you to see spirit and to see the truth in all things. Allow your third eye to open wide, just like you would your physical eyes. You are ready to receive these visions. Know that your visions will enhance your life and help others.

See your third eye open with confidence in readiness for its journey.

Say the following affirmation three times to anchor your commitment to see spirit and the truth:

Spirit of truth, come to me, show yourself, my mind is free.

Sit quietly with your eyes closed and allow any visions to come. See yourself looking through the third eye. Let the visions come and go naturally. If you see nothing, just be patient and keep looking. Relax, breathe and let the visions happen.

After approximately 10-15 minutes, whether you have seen anything or not, say:

Thank you for visiting me. Please continue to help me with my clairvoyant abilities.

Then visualize your third eye closing and returning to the oval shape. Your clairvoyant window is then closed and rested.

It's important never to skip the last step, and always to close your third eye, particularly in the early stages of development. The third eye needs to rest as you go on about your daily life. You will find as you develop that the eye tends to open more naturally and on command like a switch. But, just like a gym workout, it needs to work out at intervals, not all the time.

Write up all you experienced during the exercise. What did you see? Did you see colours or places, a house perhaps, or memories that didn't seem to belong to you? If you saw nothing, then write that down too. Just be patient and don't force anything to happen. Results can take a while, but know that they will come.

Perhaps instead of, or in addition to, seeing visions you felt a presence or sensation, or heard a voice – one of your other clairs received input. This is not uncommon, and it may indicate you are much further along in your development than you thought.

Exercise: Developing Clairaudience

Sit in a comfortable position. Close your eyes and breathe deeply in through the nose and out through the mouth. Fill your lungs as much as possible. Relax and let go of any earthly thoughts or stresses. If your thoughts wander, just bring yourself back to your breathing.

Focus on the ear chakras. See them glowing warm violet, vibrant and full of promise. Feel them warm gently as they open to hear sounds from the spirit world. Affirm to yourself:

My clairaudient ability is strengthening and opening as I activate my ear chakras to hear the voice and sounds of spirit. They open with ease as I affirm, 'Voice of spirit, do come near, so I may hear you loud and clear'.

Visualize a cone-shaped energy emitting and extending from your ears, like a hearing trumpet. This will help to detect spirit voices and hear them clearly. Leave yourself in this expanded state, ears listening, and see what you hear.

After about 15 minutes, bring your awareness back to the room. See the ear cones slowly shrink back into the ears. It's now time to return and write down anything you may have heard.

Hearing spirit voices is a profound experience. To some it may seem a little odd or weird at first, but the more you hear clairaudiently, the more natural it becomes. We are always humbled and honoured by the spirits who take their time to talk to us.

The spirit voices you hear for clairaudience will not be heard by others around you as they are not physical voices. For the most part, you will be the sole percipient of the spirit voice, and will relay what you hear to the sitters.

Listen carefully. You may just get the odd word here and there, or a phrase, and on occasion a full sentence. Some non-mediums often think it's like having a chat on your mobile phone for hours with your best friend. If only it were that simple!

Notice if there is an accent, and pay attention to the inflection or phrasing used. Are the voice and its characteristics soft or harsh, gentle or firm? What phrases or unusual wordings are being used?

Clairaudience is not limited to spirit voices. Over the years we have heard wedding bells, the happy birthday song being sung (out of tune we might add), dogs barking, bagpipes, national anthems, and angelic choral music. Our list is endless and so might be yours, as well. What could all those other sounds mean? Well, it's important always to speak out about what you hear and not edit.

For example, the birthday song might relate to the birthday of the sitter, someone close to the sitter, or the communicating spirit. Ask the spirit to clarify. Bagpipes might relate to Scotland where someone lived or had an interest, or to a musical skill someone learned. A national anthem might point to a country of origin. If you are not familiar with what you are hearing, hum it or record it and see what comes up.

Exercise: Developing Clairsentience

Borrow a watch, ring or small object you know nothing about, and from a person you do not know.

Hold the object in your hand. Some prefer to use their strong hand, the hand they write with. However, impressions seem to flow with whatever hand is used. Experiment and see if it makes a difference for you. If you are writing down your impressions as you receive them, you will want to keep your dominant hand free, of course.

Find a quiet and comfortable place to sit.

Close your eyes and visualise your sacral chakra opening with its orange glow. This will assist in feeling emotions and help you get 'gut' impressions from the object.

Follow this by opening the heart chakra, seeing its green energy radiate out. This will help you with compassion and empathy.

Once the chakras are open, breathe, relax and close your eyes. Say:

I now allow myself to feel sense the energy from this object.

You may wish to open your eyes at this point and relax into the impressions you get. If you feel you can sense more with the eyes closed, you can maintain that for now. In time, you will find that you can do it with your eyes fully open.

Whatever impressions you get, write them down or speak them out loud if you are recording. Never edit what you sense – the impressions arise for a reason, no matter how strange they might seem.

When you feel you have gotten all the information you can from the object, put it down. Take a deep breath and see you sacral and heart chakras close and return to their normal daily existence.

Share your impressions with the person who knows about the object to validate your accuracy. Don't be surprised if you bring forward some gems that are revelations for the client.

Exercise: Developing Claircognizance

Get a pen or pencil and some paper.

Sit comfortably in a chair with your writing materials on your lap or on a table. Close your eyes and use your breath, in through the nose and out through the mouth, to relax you. If thoughts wander, return your attention to your breath. Clear your mind.

When you feel focused and relaxed, ready yourself for automatic writing. Take pen or pencil in hand and mentally ask spirit a question.

Write whatever comes into your mind. Let it flow without judgment or analysis. Do not worry about 'making it up'. Let the words flow. You may be inspired to draw pictures as well.

Continue for as long as you feel the energy. Then put down your pen or pencil, close your eyes, and thank spirit for the communication.

Use your breath to refocus yourself in your seat, and return to ordinary awareness.

Review and evaluate what you wrote. Some of it may be disjointed or sound nonsensical; that's all right, as you are getting used to this mode of communication. Keep practicing, and messages will become clearer and longer.

Practice these exercises regularly and you will be well on your way to productive mediumship.

CHAPTER 7

BUILDING YOUR SPIRIT TEAM

Now we turn our focus to who your spirit allies are on the other side. We all have a team of spirit helpers and other entities who are there, if we ask, to help us and help with our unfoldment as the spiritual beings we are in truth. You may have noticed that we said, 'if we ask', for asking is of upmost importance. The universal law of free will is at play here.

Spirits, angels and the like are always present for us, but can only intervene and assist us if we ask them to – it's like giving your consent. They often step in when something serious needs to be brought to attention, but in regard to development, asking for their assistance is a must. They are there to help in any way they can, and will help you if you are pure in mind and heart and you are working in the light.

If you are overly egotistical or working for the wrong reasons, don't expect a great response from the light. You will more likely draw in lower level spirits and entities who may seem helpful at first but will soon want their pound of flesh. Like attracts like, so always work in the light with honesty and integrity. This will always pay dividends. Keep your karma balanced, and that will bring you some awesome experiences and opportunities in life.

Below you will find descriptions of some of the most common types of spiritual helpers. Some of us work with a wide array of these guides, which brings a freshness and all round balanced approach to our work. Some prefer to work only with one or two helpers, such as spirit guides or angels. There is no right or wrong; it's what works and resonates with you as an individual.

Spirit guides

Spirit guides are highly enlightened beings who have lived many lives on earth under many different circumstances. They are specialised in different areas, be it spirituality, music, art and the like.

They are given their role as a guide to you before you are born to this earth. They have an affinity to your spirit that is about to be born or reborn. They understand your predetermined path that you will follow. It doesn't mean that everything throughout your life is predetermined, or that you can't change as you walk along your path. We have all been given free will, and it is our responsibility to use that along with common sense and guided action.

Many of us have more than one guide, such as spiritual workers who work Tarot, healing, magic, mediumship and so on. These guides all have specific skills to help you along your path and to help you to become the best you can be.

Both of us have guides who work with us in our different forms of spiritual work. We, as most of you, also have one primary guide who is present and available more than the rest. Primary guides stay with you for your lifetime on earth. They draft in other experts in the spirit world if needed, much as we do here on earth.

It's not unusual to have your guides with you for many lifetimes. You may also have known your guide in a previous life where you both shared an earthly bond. We have found through our research that many variables are possible.

Whilst it's nice to believe that our favourite grandmother or funny uncle might be a spirit guide, in some cases, they really are. Many times, however, they are not guides per se, as they may not have had enough experience throughout their incarnations to have been elevated to the rank of spirit guide.

A guide has great responsibility. If you had shared a strong bond with grandma or uncle, they will be looking over you and can assist you on your path. However, we must remember that now they are in spirit, they still have learning to do themselves and must evaluate the life spent on earth in their last incarnation. If they have lived enough lives, one day they may become a guide to future generations of the family. These can be known as ancestral guides and, who knows, one day you may also be enlightened enough to join the ranks of being a spirit guide.

Angels and archangels

Angels and archangels, who are higher ranking angels, are a firm favourite with many spiritually minded people, ourselves included. The prospect of having a guardian angel is endearing and helps one feel nurtured and protected. Indeed, it should, because we all have a guardian angel and sometimes more than one. Angels are beings of love and light, lovingly created by the divine in its image, which is pure unconditional love.

Some people ask if their mum or dad have become an angel after passing, but this is not how it works. Angels are purely spiritual beings of light, who have not lived a mortal life on earth. However, in ancient lore, it is said that the prophets Elijah and Enoch were elevated to the angelic ranks to become the archangels Sandalphon and Metatron, respectively. The Book of Enoch tells in detail the story of how Enoch was called to heaven to bring the teachings of God to humanity, after which he transcended to heaven and became Metatron.

We work very closely with angels and archangels and help clients connect to them on a regular basis. We feel privileged to work closely with these beings of light who have helped us and come to our aid many times over the years. Recall our encounters with them in Chapter 1.

Angels serve as non-judgmental guides regardless of religion, colour, creed or sexual orientation. The angels are always positive in their communications with you, and will help you develop in your channelling skills so you can hear them loud and clear. Although they are beings of light, you can always rely on them for strength to overcome any adversity.

All you need to do to let the angels into your life is welcome them by saying something like, 'To my dear guardian angel or angels, I ask for you to allow me to experience your wondrous energy and to help guide me on my path of light and truth'. They will be there in an instant. Remember that you must ask any angel or guide to for their help, as they will not interfere with free will. Ask and it is given.

Ancestors and loved ones

Ancestors are great guides to get to know. They have been there, seen it and got the t-shirt.

Throughout history, many cultures have had strong spiritual practices of honouring and consulting the ancestral dead. The same is true today – we all have ancestors, even from previous lives, who are ready to aid us on life's journey. We can connect with them through meditation and past-life regression. All you have to do is call out to them and allow them to step forth and impart their wisdom.

Your loved ones are those you have loved in this lifetime: mum or dad, brother or sister, best friend and so on. They don't have to be a relation to you – just someone with whom you shared a loving bond. These loved ones are the people who were there for you on earth and were loving and supportive. Even though they are now in the spirit world, they still want to be part of your life and will assist you as much as they are permitted. They, like other guides, will not interfere in your free will and the lessons you still to learn. As with all spiritual beings we must ask for their help first.

We can maintain strong bonds to our ancestors and other loved ones by keeping their memories alive through cherished mementoes. Many individuals keep personal altars at home, where they place photographs, personal possessions and so on.

One powerful way to connect with the ancestral dead and loved ones from this lifetime is an event called the 'dumb supper'. The dumb supper evolved out of old folklore divination practices. The old rituals called for serving a meal at midnight. A place was always set for the dead as an invitation to be present. The meal was eaten in silence and in reverse order, that is, a sweet or dessert was served first and the main course or a starter was served last. All food was served to the dead. The participants hoped that the dead would appear and give predictions, especially concerning the future husbands of the girls present.

Today the practice, growing in popularity, is done for remembrance and honouring the dead. Dumb suppers follow the old tradition of eating in silence in reverse order. We always start with a prayer to set the mood and to evoke our ancestors. We eat in silence so we can think about our ancestors and loved ones in spirit, not in a sad, melancholy way but in a celebratory way. We think about how they walked our path before and how they may want to be able to help us now.

The dumb supper is an event everyone should try at some point. You can even do an informal version – simply set a place at your table and serve the same food you are eating. Your ancestors and loved ones will join you in a meal of celebration and honour.

Spirit animals and familiars

Animal guides go by many names depending on tradition and culture. Feel free to use what resonates with you. Most people, certainly spiritual people, love animal guides in all their forms, whether it's a purring cat on your lap or a majestic fox who appears and disappears seemingly at random.

One of the first questions many people ask is, does the animal have to be living to be a guide or assistant to you as medium? The short answer is, it depends on your own circumstance.

We had a beautiful little cat named Demoose. She was such a dear and precious little girl, always there to give love, and she had such a magical energy about her. She would often meditate with us, lying still next to us and only moving when we had finished. In 2007, she passed away at only 4 years old from a blood clot. Although it has been sad not to have her physically around us, she continues to make her presence known to us. She is around when we give private readings and healings to clients, and even around us as we are writing this book.

Whether the animal is a pet or favourite wild animal, whether they are physically here or in spirit, they can still assist you. Just sit quietly and think of the animal in question, even if they are not present, and you will link on to the essence of that beautiful creature and blend with its energy.

Other types of guides

There are endless possibilities for 'Team Spirit.' You must commune with whatever guides or helpers you feel akin to. This can be dependent on your own spiritual or religious background, or perhaps you may have an agnostic or eclectic approach to the way you express yourself. There is no right or wrong or 'one better than the other' scenario, for they all bring guidance and protection. Just as in life, we have best friends, close friends, friends, acquaintances, work colleagues and so on. That can be the same with your spirit team. Work with whom you feel drawn to and build a relationship of trust and respect from that.

Better still, allow them to introduce themselves to you. Use discernment in all situations, and above all, feel happy with who you wish to be guided by. You are always in control because of the law of free will.

CHAPTER 8

MEDITATION: THE KEY TO THE OTHER SIDE

If you want to build a strong link to the spirit world, you should consider following a regular practice of meditation. Mediation helps us explore not only spirit, but our true selves too. It clears the mind of clutter and chatter, and sharpens our focus and concentration, not only to spirit communication but in all areas of the life.

Meditation is clinically proven to lower blood pressure, alleviate stress, clear brain fog and enhance well-being. Life can be busy and demanding. Work and family life, socials with friends, and an endless bombardment of social media can leave us fatigued by the end of the day. If you try to contact spirit when you are fraught with the day's events, it will seem an arduous task which will only tire you further. Being in the right mind-set for contact is of upmost importance and will produce the best results.

There are many different types of meditation, and we urge you to sample some so that you can find what's right for you. Traditional meditation, such as taught in Eastern spirituality, is an emptying of the mind, and is practiced with the goal of union with the godhead or Absolute. Some of these states of meditation are quite deep, like trance.

There is another form of meditation, active meditation, that is much more popular in the West. It employs visualisations, dialogue and affirmations, and is goal-oriented. Active meditation does involve letting go of distracting thoughts so the voice of spirit can come through. The meditator uses specific images, thoughts and intentions to focus on the goal. In active meditation, you are always conscious, but in a pleasant and light altered state.

Many people work with both forms of meditation, as they both have their unique benefits.

We share with you now simple yet highly effective visualisation meditations that have served us and our students well over the years. You close your eyes and visualise according to the guidance. Relax into the experience and go deeper into your subconscious mind. Allow the guided thoughts and visualisations to take shape whilst you remain unaware of earthly concerns around you. It's like a mini vacation – sounds nice just reading about it, doesn't it?

Meditation preparation checklist

For best results:

- Make sure you will not be disturbed.

- Make sure that all mobile and landline phones are on silent.

- Make sure you are in a place where you feel comfortable and safe, such as your own home.

- If you are going to play music, select a neutral piece without lyrics. You don't want any music that could make you think, 'I've heard this before' or 'I like those words'. Lyrics can also evoke memories that interfere in the meditation.

- If you burn incense, essential oils or a fragranced candle, make sure they are safely placed so not to cause fire or injury. If you are not familiar with the properties of essential oils, consult an expert such as an aromatherapist.

- Set yourself a time limit of say, 30-45 minutes or an hour at tops, and set a 'gentle alarm call' if need be. You can use your cell phone (if the alarm still sounds whilst on silent) or other type of device. Make sure the volume is down low as you don't want to be startled out of meditation.

Now you are all set for your meditation. Below you will find two guided meditation exercises that will help you expand yourself and your own personal spiritual power. It is like taking your car for a service and having it finely tuned. Your car always responds better after a tune up and your mediumship can flourish in the same way after your meditative tune up.

As with the other exercises in this book, we recommend sitting in a comfortable position rather than lying down. No matter what your resolve, it is often hard not to fall asleep.

Blending with the Power

'Blending with the Power' is one of our personal favourites, and is one of the most powerful ways to strengthen psychic and mediumistic channels. We were inspired by a similar meditation exercise that was taught to us by the English medium Glyn Edwards, who Dean mentioned in Chapter 1, and we decided to create our own version.

This is not a meditation about connecting with spirit in a direct way, but is more about expanding your own spirit through the use of nature's energy. By recognising and strengthening your own spirit, you soon come to realise that your very own spirit that is encased in your physical body can attune with other energies in an easy, yet profound way. This builds confidence and will help you trust what messages you receive from spirit.

Exercise: Blending with the Power

Sit in a comfortable position, upright with your hands resting in your lap.

Become aware of yourself breathing in and out, in through the nose and out through the mouth. Focus on this controlled and rhythmic breathing. After around seven or eight controlled breaths, allow yourself to come back to a comfortable level of breathing. If your mind wanders at any time just bring your focus back on to your breathing.

With each in breath feel an expansion of your spirit. It will feel like an energy from within that grows in size and power. On the out breath relax. Again, breathe in to expand your spirit and relax on the out breath. Keep repeating, and pay attention to your expansion.

As you expand further, feel your energy fill the room, almost touching the walls. Know that you can expand beyond this to the outside environment. Your spirit energy has no boundaries – it is limitless energy and the most powerful thing we have access and control over.

Now expand your energy outside, to the immediate surroundings, or even somewhere else outside. Allow your spirit to take you on this journey and go with the flow, knowing you are totally safe and being nurtured all the time.

Shift your awareness outside. Do you feel the sun on your face or a cool breeze with the full moon shining her majestic light on you? Feel the grass under your feet, smell the natural scent of nature. See yourself surrounded by the bright colours in nature. Smell the flowers, plants and trees. Know that everything in nature has powerful energy. Allow that energy to blend with your own.

Look at the sky and continue your journey to a mountain with snowy caps. Feel that elevation and know that your power is growing with each experience.

Visit a beautiful sandy beach and watch as the waves gently dance. Look as the tide ebbs and flows. Use this as a metaphor that energy ebbs and flows and now it is time to let go and flow with those energies, knowing that it is indeed safe to do that. Don't swim against the tide in your development, but go with the flow. It will always lead you to where you need to be with your development, and lead you to what you must become.

Rest in this expanded state. Then return your consciousness to your seated position and use your breath to ground and centre the body.

You can vary this exercise by continuing the journey, visiting other places in the natural world, perhaps majestic waterfalls, ancient forests and even the depths of the ocean. They too hold great natural power which, when blended with yours, provides the most exquisite experiences. One of the most important things with this exercise is to sense and visualise your personal journey. This empowers you and will garnish great results for use in mediumship and in your wider world in general.

Spirit guide meditation

We have been using the following meditation for many years with great success. We first created this in our early days of development and we now share it with you for the first time in print. Its purpose is to find out who your spirit guide or guides is/are. This is one of the first questions many psychic mediums are asked. All of us have spirit guides, without question, as we discussed in Chapter 7. This meditation will help you identify them and build a good relationship with them.

You will need a writing pad and pen or pencil nearby to record your experiences straight after the meditation.

Exercise: Meeting Your Spirit Guide

Find yourself a comfortable place to sit upright with your hands in your lap. Relax every part of your body, beginning at the head. Feel your head, neck and shoulders relax, allowing any tension to melt away. Allow your spine and hips to feel relaxed and supported in the chair. Let your legs, knees and ankles feel heavy and relaxed. Let your feet feel like they are on cotton wool and so comfortable.

Building a relationship with your spirit guide can bring wonderful results to your mediumistic and psychic development.

Take some deep cleansing breaths, in through the nose and out through the mouth. Do seven or eight repetitions and then return breathing back to normal.

Find yourself walking down a country lane surrounded by lush green trees. Feel the breeze on your face and the warmth of the sun beaming its healing rays upon you, filling you with vitality and a sense of wonder.

You feel very relaxed and weightless, and you feel a positivity like never before.

At the end of this country lane you see an archway. It looks like the ruins of some enchanted castle in a timeless story. It is inviting and you slowly approach it, admiring its beauty along the way. It has beautiful jade green ivy climbing it. You know that by stepping through you will experience something profound and life-changing.

You now step through his arch with excitement. Find yourself standing at the top of an ancient staircase. You feel drawn to descend the stairs, very slowly, knowing something wonderful awaits. There are 10 steps, and with each step down, you feel more and more deeply relaxed, peaceful and serene. You arrive at your last step and find yourself in an enchanted garden, feeling peaceful and calm.

Look around the garden. It is blooming with colour? See the flowers, bright yellows, healing blues and energetic reds all shimmering in the bright sunshine. The bees are busy pollinating and the gentle breeze makes the flowers dance and the trees whistle. The birdsong you hear is almost angelic and makes you feel so alive and loved.

You become aware of the sound of running water, a gentle babbling brook. You look across to the other side of the garden and see a little bridge across the babbling brook. You decide to walk over to this beautifully inviting place. As you approach, you see the bridge has a bench halfway across it. You feel inspired to sit on this bench with the gentle, healing waters representing your emotions and intuition flowing beneath you.

As you sit quietly on the bench, listening to the relaxing sounds of the water, you notice a figure standing at the foot of the other side of the bridge. You look at the figure. You feel a familiarity and are comfortable in their presence. This is your spirit guide waiting to meet you. Notice as much detail as you can. Are they male or female? What are the hair and features like, and what clothes are they wearing?

Smile over at the figure and silently ask them to join you on the bench. You feel safe, calm and nurtured by this whole experience. It's like meeting with an old friend.

Mentally ask your guide for their name and wait for the answer. Whatever comes through, accept that as their answer. It may be a name that is popular and well-known today or it could be a name that you've never heard. Accept that you have been given an answer. If you get no response straight away, just be patient and trust that it will come, because it will.

Now that you've been formally introduced, sit quietly and ask any questions you may have, such as, 'How long have you been my guide'? You may get the answer of 'many lifetimes', which can explain the familiarity that you feel – you have met before. Another question might be, 'What is my next step to development'? And so on.

Allow your guide to impart whatever wisdom they see fit, as they always know what you need to know at that time. When you feel that enough time has elapsed, thank your guide for being present with you and for the wisdom that they have imparted.

It is now time to journey back. You look around the sacred garden and admire its beauty once more. As you look to the other side of the garden you can see the 10 steps that brought you down to this enchanted place. You feel ready to climb those steps again on your journey home.

You find yourself at the bottom step and begin to climb. As you climb, you feel more and more energy entering your body. You feel full of vitality and ready to take on the world in a happy, peaceful and positive way.

You arrive at the tenth and top step feeling fantastic. You look at the arch that brought you on this journey and step through with vigour. You walk back along the country lane at a brisk pace.

Then slowly feel yourself sitting in the chair back in your room. Bring your focus to your breathing once more and when you feel ready, open your eyes.

Get your notepad and pen and write up your experience in as much detail as possible, including what the garden looked like, the appearance of your guide, the name, and all other meaningful pieces of information. Be as descriptive as possible and keep as many records you can, especially in the early stages of development. When you look back on them in years to come you can see how much your practice evolved and changed.

It's nice and most appropriate in your awakened state to give thanks or gratitude for your whole experience. I have always shown my gratitude and appreciation to spirit every time in practice, whether it be a demonstration, reading, workshop or mediation. Not only is it polite to do so, but it helps deepen the bond with spirit and shows your appreciation that you take nothing for granted.

CHAPTER 9

TOOLS OF SPIRIT COMMUNICATION

In this chapter, we explore the different types of tools that can be employed for effective and safe communication with the spirit world. In truth, we have found through our own experience over the years that mediums themselves are the best tool for bringing forth some of the best evidence. Nonetheless, many mediums like to work with tools as an aid – they help to stimulate the flow of energy and information, and boost the process. In addition, tools augment training to bring forth your natural mediumistic gifts.

The tools featured here are by no means exhaustive; they are ones we have used over the years with great success. Some are ancient, used by many for centuries, and others are more modern and techy, but nonetheless produce results. You may ask, how do you measure success using such tools? The answer is, it's all in the quality of the evidence. Quality evidence brought through by spirit is something that can be understood and recognised by the receiver. We mean specifics such as names, dates, addresses, places, and details about the communicating personality.

Whilst reading our list of tools, see what resonates with you and what you feel drawn to try. Pick one and experiment with it. Document everything you do and experiment. Over time you may decide to give them all a try, along with other tools not listed here.

Preparation for working with tools

Whichever tools you chose to work with, it's important to follow a few simple rules. These are in place to help your session be safe and effective. They set the scene and allow spirit to know that you are ready to communicate.

- Chose a place where you will not be disturbed.

- Set a regular time for your work. Spirit doesn't work on linear time, but we do, and they get to know when we are available.

- Turn off your mobile/cell phone or put it on silent or vibrate. The energy given off a mobile phone, even if it's inaudible, is capable of unbalancing the energy in the room, which in turn lessens the energy of spirit presence. Thus, you may want to keep your phone out of the room altogether.

- Show respect! We all like to be given respect, and spirit expects the same.

- Be serious. Approach this with a positive and serious attitude. Do not embark on this amazing journey just for laughs, to impress friends, or use as a common parlour entertainment. This is a fascinating subject that can change your thoughts and enhance your life.

- Open and close each session with a prayer or affirmation. An affirmation, you recall, is a positive sentiment or statement. Tailor it to what you will be doing. It focuses your intention on what you are seeking to accomplish. Here is an example:

I open this session to communicate with spirits from the light and ask for protection from my guides.

Similarly, when you finish the session close it with:

Thank you spirits for attending this session, I/we now ask you to return to your place in peace and to leave our environment.

Create your own affirmations for your specific purposes. Affirmations are powerful, and they reap great rewards.

- Be open-minded, otherwise you will limit your own psychic ability and will produce weak results, if any. There's plenty of time to assess and evaluate after the event, but for now just be in the present and be open to the wonders of spirit communication.

- Do not drink alcohol or use recreational drugs before or during the session. Alcohol and drugs create gaps and weaknesses in your aura that will attract lower spirits interested in exploiting your vulnerabilities.

The Ouija/Spirit Board

'Oh no,' we hear you cry, 'I would never use one of those.' Just relax.

This popular tool goes by many names: spirit board, witch board, talking board, and its trademarked name, Ouija. A board may be made of wood, slate, stone, marble, composite materials, and even cardboard. Boards feature the letters of the alphabet, numbers 0 through 9, and words such as 'yes', 'no', 'hello' and 'goodbye'. Some are beautiful and ornate and some are very plain.

The board has a mysterious history. It was created in the late nineteenth century by toy manufacturers in Baltimore, Maryland in the US. They were intrigued by the enormous popularity of the planchette and the dial plate, especially being used in séances and Spiritualism circles in Ohio, and wanted to exploit this popularity in a commercial way.

The planchette in use then was a small wooden platform with three legs, two of which had small wheels and one of which was a pencil. Users placed their fingertips lightly on the planchette and asked spirit to write out messages.

The dial plate was a large wheel that resembled a roulette wheel, but with letters and numbers on the rim. It was mounted and could be spun for the spelling-out of messages.

The Ouija adapted both ideas. The board replaced the dial plate, and the planchette had three legs but no pencil. Users placed their hands lightly on the planchette, and supposedly spirit would push the planchette around to point at letters, numbers and words. Thus, spirit could use the board to spell messages.

The US patent for the Ouija was issued in 1891, and the first commercially sold boards soon followed. The Ouija was intended for entertainment, and to take advantage of popular interest in spirit

*The Ouija board, often misunderstood, is still hugely popular as a tool
for connecting with spirit.*

communication. Now a person could consult the spirits in their own
home, without having to visit a professional medium or attend a spirit
circle or séance.

The Ouija was a huge success and spawned imitations, all of
which were eventually crushed by the shrewd marketing of William

105

Fuld, who took over the company from the original founders, and whose name is still on the board today.

As for the origin of the name 'Ouija', Fuld deliberately promoted mystery around it. One story held that the name was a combination of the French and German words for 'yes', respectively *oui* and *ja*. Actually, the original founders asked the board what it should be called, and it gave that answer. One of the participants at that session was the sister of one of the founders, a woman who had natural mediumistic ability. She was wearing a necklace that said OUIJA on it. Did that have any influence on what was spelled out on the board? No one knows which came first.

The Ouija rose to become one of the top-selling game boards; many millions of them have been sold. Critics scowl darkly about the board being marketed as a toy, but this has to do with the US Internal Revenue Service. The original manufacturers contended the board was exempt from taxation because it was a 'spiritual' device, but the IRS held it to be a taxable game. In 1920, the IRS won, and that is why the board is a 'game' and a 'toy' today in the US. In the UK only specialist shops stock them.

The Ouija has gone through several changes of ownership and today is owned by the toy giant Hasbro, Inc.

This tool has gotten a bad press over the years and not all of it is justified. Hollywood films in particular have used it as a demonic device for evil spirits to manipulate as a way of acting out in the material world, terrorising and even killing people. We must leave the Hollywood misconception of it being a portal to evil at the door.

All tools are neutral, and the Ouija is no different. The tool itself is just that, a tool, nothing more, nothing less. When you buy them from your store or on the internet they don't generally come with spirits attached to them.

Because of the sensational reputation of the Ouija, many users, especially young people, misuse it for thrills. No wonder they run the risk of an unpleasant experience. Any tool used in that manner would open the door to the same.

It's how you use the tool, not the tool itself, that determines what happens with it. Many millions of people all over the world have used a Ouija or spirit board without a problem, but there have indeed been cases where the board seems to have unleashed some unsavoury being upon the players. Those cases receive an exaggerated amount of publicity, causing people to think that *all* spirit boards are bad, and any use of one will invite trouble. It's like saying you would never fly on a plane because it might crash, even though the odds against it are quite high.

The likelihood of you encountering a negative issue with a Ouija or spirit board is very remote. We have been present at many spirit board sessions, including using one, and have never experienced anything malign. The choice is of course yours to make. If you feel nervous or reluctant to use a Ouija or spirit board, then choose other tools instead.

As you will recall from Chapter 1, my (Stuart) experiences as a child may seem scary to some, and I admit that at times they were a little unnerving. I want to underline here that using the board in my childhood home did not bring 'something' into the house. It was already there, lying in wait to communicate. We had used a board to reach out to this spirit, and it answered. The phenomena may have continued in exactly the same fashion without the use of a Ouija board. Using the board actually may have helped things stay a little calmer, as this spirit, even though darker in nature, was able to vent its thoughts and feelings.

There are many schools of opinion on the Ouija; we just want people to look at things from all angles. Over the years of using the board, we've seen some good evidence, and healing experiences for many observers and sitters. If you follow these rules and come up with some of your own to feel extra secure, then you should experience good and evidential sessions.

How to use the board

Never use the board alone. There is a strength in numbers, and it's also important that you have someone who can corroborate your experiences if they are not just subjective in nature. In an ideal scenario two people work the board, a third person makes notes of what the board is saying, and if there's a fourth person, they can keep their eye on the board, room and participants to ensure everything is going well. Sometimes the fourth person records the session with a camera, video cam, and/or digital recorder.

If there are only two persons present, it's a good idea to record the session on a digital recorder so that you do not have to be concerned with remembering all the details as you go along. Sometimes the planchette moves with surprising speed.

Prepare your questions to start the session. They should be serious and not of a frivolous nature. Don't ask questions such as the winning numbers for the next lottery, is so-and-so having an affair, or when you are going to die. Keep them light, meaningful, and for the benefit of all in attendance.

Prior to a session, cleanse the board of previous energies. Even new boards should be initiated with a cleansing, to clear away any residues from manufacturing and handling. Use a smudge stick of sage, which can be purchased online or at a spiritual-themed store. Light the stick and waft the smoke about the board saying:

This sacred smoke does cleanse this board and draws in only light and love, this spirit board is now all cleansed for communing with those above.

For the exercise below, a drinking glass can be substituted for the planchette. The planchette has a clear plastic window. For correctly determining spellings, the window or glass must be centred over a letter, number or word.

Exercise: Using A Ouija or Spirit Board

Gain rapport with the planchette by placing your fingers lightly on the board. Move planchette in a circle or in a numeral eight lying sideways, which is the symbol of infinity.

Once you feel connected, breathe deeply and relax and become at one with the board and planchette. The more you and the participants are relaxed and focused, the more the session will flow.

Double check that everyone present, including yourself, feels ready to embark on this journey. Anyone who is not fully in the moment, or has any last-minute doubts or anxieties, should be excused from the session. Ask them to sit outside the room, as anyone with severe nerves can hinder the communication. It is quite normal for the inexperienced to feel a little nervous or anxious, but if this becomes extreme, then the session will not flow and the enjoyment for other participants will be spoiled.

Offer a prayer for protection. Whatever you choose is appropriate. No single prayer is better than others. A prayer, like an affirmation, sets intention and allows the spirit world to know that you are ready for communication.

A simple, generic prayer that covers all grounds and doesn't use a particular deity is something like this:

We ask for protection from the highest beings and universal powers of positivity. Encircle us with love, light and protection only allowing spirits with the best intent to communicate with us.

Rest your fingertips lightly on the planchette and ask if there is a spirit presence who wishes to communicate with you. Always be respectful to the spirits as you would a physical person. The rule of thumb is, 'Treat them how you would like to be treated'. Do not taunt or provoke.

Allow the planchette to glide over the letters, numbers and words. Never push or will it to say a certain thing. Let spirit guide you.

Ask questions, and if there are no answers or nonsensical responses, move on to other questions. Sometimes the board has to 'warm up'. We have known spirits on the board to find lost objects and give accurate family details when the usual method of ancestry searches has turned up nothing.

The messages from spirit should always be of a helpful nature. Remember that you, not spirit, is always in control of the session. If negative or nasty comments come from the board, immediately stop the session. Move the planchette to the goodbye position and say:

We now end this session and close the door on you now, you are not welcome. Good by'!

If there are no problems, enjoy the session, and allow it to continue no more than 20 to 30 minutes. Board sessions take more energy than you might realise.

A 20- to 30-minute session should provide enough information for all participants to discuss.

To close the session and the spirit door, thank all spirits for coming through, such as:

We thank you spirits for communicating with us and we ask that you now return and leave us, going with our love and gratitude. The session is now closed. Blessings to all.

Afterwards, everyone should discuss what transpired during the session. This processing is important so that everyone feels complete and comfortable, so make sure you provide the time for it. Discuss what came through the board and also how people felt. Did participants experience anything physical, such as their hair or face being stroked; warm or cold sensations; unexplained breezes or noises, etc.? It's important to share these, as you will be surprised just how many may have experienced the same phenomena. It is a nice validation.

Making your own spirit communication board

You can easily make an inexpensive spirit board. Why would you make one instead of buying a commercial one? Sometimes you need a board on short notice for an impromptu session and none are available. In other cases, some individuals feel that a homemade board is more effective because it contains their personal energy. Both commercial and homemade boards get results. Remember, it's the users who determine the nature of a session and its results, not the tool.

111

Just four items will help you make a fully functioning board:

- Packs of sticky memo notes or small square pieces of card approximately 3x3 inches square, plus three slightly longer pieces 3x5 inches

- A thick marker or pen

- A small, freshly washed glass

- A medium to large table, round or square

Cut 36 pieces of card or paper into even sizes, or use sticky memo notes if you have them. On these pieces write the 26 letters of the alphabet and on the remaining 10 the numbers 0-9.

Now cut three slightly larger pieces (3x5) of paper and write; Yes, No and Goodbye on them.

Some add Maybe as a fourth, but we think that word is too ambiguous when it comes to communicating with spirit. Some also add Good and Evil. We don't think we need to do that as we are all working in the light and have prepared and protected ourselves accordingly. Plus, it's unlikely that any potential spirit or entity that starts communicating will announce itself as evil.

On the table, evenly space all the alphabetised pieces of paper in a clockwise position, so that 'A' would be at 1 o'clock and so on. Now add the numbers to the circle. Place Yes and No at 10 and 2 o'clock, respectively, and finally place Goodbye at 6 o'clock. Make sure they are all evenly spaced but not overlapping, which could lead to confused messages.

Put the glass on the table inverted so fingers can rest on the top, which is the bottom of the glass. Use the glass as you would a planchette. Keep your fingers lightly on it, and do not push or press. Some say that spirit energy builds inside the glass, which enables it to move, and we have found that this can indeed be the case. Allow the glass indicator to glide over the table and to the letters, words or numbers as you would a traditional board.

You can get some great messages from a homemade board. Remember, our ancestors would have used similar methods before the advent of the marketed board.

The Dark Mirror

For centuries across the globe, shiny surfaces and mirrors have been doorways to the spirit world and an easy way to journey to the world beyond. Mirror-gazing and crystal-gazing are two popular techniques that have a long, honoured history.

The dark or black mirror is a tool that we use all the time in a technique known as 'scrying', which means 'to catch sight of' or 'to discern dimly'. It derives from the Middle English *descry*, meaning 'to describe'. Throughout history people have used all kinds of reflective surfaces for scrying, the best-known of which is probably the crystal ball. However, dark shiny surfaces have been favoured by many – a preference dating to thousands of years ago when black shiny stones served the purpose to part the veil.

Today a dark mirror is a piece of glass that has been ritually prepared and painted black on one side then framed for working. By gazing into the dark reflective surface, the third eye is stimulated, and one may see, hear, sense and feel communicators from spirit.

Some dark mirrors are made of natural stone, such as polished, flat and smooth obsidian or Whitby jet, which create a similar effect. Dark bowls filled with water or ink, dark ponds, and so on work as well, as long as the water or liquid is still and not rippling or running.

Does size matter? Size is a personal preference – bigger is not necessarily better – but we have found that some sizes are too small to be effective. For example, obsidian should be at least 4 to 5 inches square or in diameter if round. Obsidian is beautiful and has a silky look, but it can also come with a hefty price tag. Tumble stones are just too small to produce good results.

All of the above variations offer excellent ways to scry, but there is nothing better, in our opinion, than an ornately framed dark mirror blessed for its primary purpose.

We have used scrying with dark mirrors for years with great success, journeying through the mirror and communicating with our loved ones, spirit guides, angels and even our beautiful cats who have crossed beyond the veil.

Our experience with dark mirrors was taken to a deeper and more profound experience when we booked a workshop called *Portal to the Spirit World - Through the Necromanteum*, hosted by the world's leading authority on the paranormal and metaphysical, Rosemary Ellen Guiley. Rosemary is a prolific author of nearly 70 books on spiritual and paranormal topics that give the reader a well-grounded insight in the spiritual realms.

We attended the workshop in the wonderful bewitching city of Salem, Massachusetts, the perfect setting for all things spiritual and paranormal. The event was a powerhouse of activity, uniting the experienced and novice in a profound journey through the dark mirror. We urge anyone to attend this annual workshop, which Rosemary conducts in other locations as well. Visit Rosemary's website at: www.visionaryliving.com.

The easiest and most cost-effective way to scry is to get yourself a purpose-made scrying mirror. Rosemary and her husband, Joe Redmiles, hand-make wonderful mirrors under the full moon, bathing them in sacred sound and healing energy, thus creating a powerful tool. We have two and love them. Rosemary's how-to guidebook, *The Art of Black Mirror Scrying*, is available online and is an in-depth look at this practice. We highly recommend you get a copy today.

The dark mirror, a time-honoured tool, can help you journey to the world beyond.

Other artisans make black mirrors as well, which you may find online or in specialty shops.

Many people who use the mirror find it to be accessible, user-friendly, and probably one of the simplest methods of spirit communication. You can do mirror work on your own or in a group, with each having their own mirror or tool of choice. Everyone will have their own personal, subjective experience. There will always be similarities, of course.

Below we offer some helpful tips for getting the most from a dark mirror.

Exercise: How to Use a Dark Mirror for Scrying

Select a place where you can work in dim light, regardless of time of day or night. Do not work in total darkness, as you need to see the surface of the mirror. Dim light helps to fatigue the physical eyes and allows the third eye to take over. A candle placed in the corner of the room behind you can work, or use an electric candle for a safer alternative. Ensure the light is not directly reflected in the mirror.

Sit quietly and undisturbed, focus on the breath and centre yourself.

Say a prayer or affirmation for protection and setting of intention.

Think of a loved one you would like to communicate with and hold them in your mind and heart. Visualise them with as much detail and heart-felt emotion as possible.

Position the mirror so you cannot see your own reflection in the surface. This is easily done by tilting the mirror if it is stood up with its own easel, or by lying it flat. The surface should look like a blank, dark screen.

Take a deep breath and ask for your loved one or guides to come through and help you journey to the world beyond. Imagine the mirror as a gateway or doorway.

Close your eyes and let yourself go into a light meditation for five minutes or so, then open your eyes and gaze softly into the mirror. Have no expectations. Allow thoughts, images, sounds and feelings to arise. Some of them will seem to emanate from, or be anchored in, the mirror, while others will be presented as an interior experience. Do not judge or analyse.

Some people get profound results right away, while others have to practice for a while to get the flow going. Do not be discouraged if nothing happens at first.

Some say that they can see the image of the intended loved one smiling back at them, while others don't see anything but have a sense that their loved one is present. If you see a strong image in the mirror, it is usually not physical, i.e., something others can see, but is most probably objective clairvoyance. Objective clairvoyance is a projection from the third eye that gives the appearance of the physical apparition. In contrast, subjective clairvoyance is something seen in your mind's eye.

Whatever you see or don't see, just relax. Remember, trying too hard interferes with results — just like when you can't sleep, the more you try the more awake you become. Allow the process to unfold naturally.

End the session when you feel fatigued, or the energy

diminishes. Thirty minutes should be ample. Return your consciousness fully to your body by using the breath to centre and ground you. Give thanks to the spirit/s you blended with and bring yourself to a waking conscious level, feeling wonderful, and knowing and believing in what you just experienced.

Keep a journal of everything you experienced, including date, time, moon phase, how you entered the meditation, how you felt as you journeyed, who you communicated with, and what the messages were. When you look back at this journey you can keep track of how your experiences and skills evolve.

Table Tipping

Table tipping, or tilting, was hugely popular during the Victorian era, from the romantically decorated séance rooms in London to the more rural areas of North America. We are pleased to say that it's made a huge comeback in recent years.

Table tipping is an art and certainly not a parlour trick. However, as in all professions some people exploit this tool with tricks to gain financial reward or publicity. Nowadays people are much more savvy, and can recognise the good from the bad.

In my early days as a medium, I (Stuart) was invited to a séance with the focus on table tipping. I'd briefly heard of this technique and never thought it could be possible... how wrong I was.

I went to a private home of a friend I'd met in circle in Kent, England. Her aunt was a medium and wanted me and a select few people to attend to experiment with table tipping. Four of us, myself included, sat around a card table waiting for further instruction from the medium, who was not at the table but watching and guiding us fledgling mediums.

Being an inquisitive person, I asked if I might examine the table before we started. The medium looked at me with a frosty yet understanding look and agreed. I just needed to satisfy my curiosity that the table wasn't rigged in any way (not that I expected this). I was glad to see that the table was just a table.

We rubbed powder into our hands at the fingertips to ensure that any grip on the table was impossible, and to soak up perspiration from the energy generated by working with spirit in this fashion. The medium asked us to place our hands lightly on the table top, and led us in prayer and evoked spirit.

She asked for spirit to make themselves known by moving the table or making a tapping sound. Within a minute the table started to vibrate. We all looked at each other with amazement. 'Can you feel something'? asked the medium. Everyone nodded in silence.

The vibrations continued to get stronger until they suddenly stopped. Then we experienced the true power of spirit. The table began to tilt.

First, the table began tilting towards me, balancing on two legs, then went to my friend. The medium had silently asked who was going to work professionally as mediums, and the table had tilted to me and my friend, Claire. Both of us went on to work professionally.

Since my introduction, we have used table tipping hundreds of times, in demonstrations, workshops and for our own research. We have a small group we work with regularly, producing incredible results. We no longer use card tables, however; we now have a beautiful antique oak table, very heavy and solid. The table moves across the floor with ease during a session, but once the session is finished it is very hard to move the table at all because of it weight. It goes to show that spirit can make something heavy move with ease.

Table tipping is probably the easiest form of physical spirit communication. It is an excellent tool for eliminating scepticism and doubts, because it is physically experienced and witnessed by everyone present. It is a fun, safe and enlightening practice. The key is to work with a good group of positive people whom you trust.

Exercise: Table Tipping

Acquire a card or wooden table. Square is better than round, for you will find the table will rise on two legs and even one leg, sometimes at extreme angles. This practice is about the physical aspect of spirit blending and working with you to create something special.

Gather four or so people you trust and who are serious about the practice.

Use talc on finger tips, which stops any grip on the table and helps prevent moisture in the fingertips.

Sit in comfortable, high backed chairs. Dining chairs are good for this. Sit close to the table so you don't have to over stretch. Only fingertips should be placed on the table. If you must rest hands on the table do so lightly.

Say your prayer of protection and evoke spirit, stating why you have gathered. Spirit will know already, but this helps to unite the consciousness of the group.

Ask for spirit to make themselves known and to use the group's collective spiritual energy to move the table.

Be patient. Sometimes it can take a few sessions before anything happens.

Ask questions throughout if you wish. The table will sometimes rap or knock. Instruct it to do once for yes

---

> and twice for no. Or, ask the table to tilt if the answer is yes.
>
> As always, be respectful and thank spirit for attending and working with you.

Write down all your experiences and share and debrief as a group.

The Séance Trumpet

The séance trumpet is another tool that has had a resurgence in the last 10 years or so. It is not like a trumpet from a brass band. It is usually constructed of thick cardboard, occasionally of aluminium. It is cone-shaped with a luminescent band painted around the wide end of the cone. The reason for the luminescent paint is that trance séances are done in total darkness, and the luminescent band helps us to see if the trumpet moves with spirit help.

The purpose of the trumpet is to help amplify any spirit voices that materialise during the séance, so they can be heard better by the sitters. It usually sits on a table with the small end up, or it can be laid prone so the sounds can flow more easily through it. We have only ever once seen a trumpet roll over during a séance. No one was near it, and a strange audible, breathy sound seemed to emit from it.

Another interesting way trumpets can be employed is during trance mediumship. The medium has the trumpet held to their voice box to allow spirit voices to be amplified.

Trumpets are not common séance and spirit communication tools. However, they can be the basis for some interesting experiments. You can purchase trumpets online made by various individuals. Aluminium trumpets from Victorian days are expensive and auctioned on sites like ebay. Replica aluminium trumpets are available from Spiritualist sources.

Pendulums

A pendulum is a weighted object on a chain or cord that is used in divination for yes and no answers to questions. It operates on the principle that it becomes an extension of a person's psychic faculty, and as a means for spirit to communicate. Using a pendulum – called dowsing – was popular during the Middle Ages as a tool for finding underground water sources where wells were then dug. Today it is used for communication with the spirit world, in matters of physical and spiritual health and well-being, and even in the commercial world as a tool for finding oil and gas resources.

The pendulum is held still, suspended at the end of its cord, and a yes-no question is asked. The answer depends on the motion of the pendulum. For example, if the pendulum starts to spin in a clockwise circle, the answer might be yes.

A pendulum can be made of any kind of material. Crystals and stones are popular. Pieces of metal work as well. In England, conkers, nuts which are encased in spikey green shells, fall from the horse chestnut tree in early autumn. They are still a popular choice used for homemade pendulums. On many a chilly Sunday afternoon, families will go out with their children and collect bags of them.

When I (Stuart) was a child, I always looked forward to autumn. I loved the darker nights, chills in the air, and coloured leaves falling majestically through the morning mist onto the dew-covered ground beneath. My family, friends and I collected conkers. We would ask an adult to pierce a conker from top to bottom, then get a shoelace and thread it through, tie it off in a knot and *voilà!* the conker became a pendulum.

Most children, however, used conkers like toys, flicking them at each other, knocking them together until they shattered, and seeing whose conker lasted the longest. I, however, had other plans.

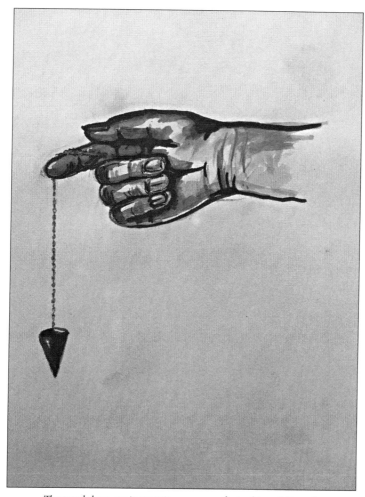

*The pendulum, an inconspicuous gem of a tool in spirit work,
can be taken anywhere.*

I was a very intuitive child and knew conkers could be used to connect with spirit, even though I did not know exactly what a pendulum was. I felt I could find out yes or no answers to questions. Don't ask me how I knew, I just knew. I would go into my grandmother's garden with my conker pendulum and ask questions. They were nothing life-changing, just regular things kids ask such as, 'Will Becky come out and play later'? or 'Will I get the Christmas present that I want'?

I would lie down and dangle the homemade pendulum over the pathway to watch for the answer. I intuitively knew that a clockwise motion meant yes and counter clockwise no. I would always trust the answers and invariably they would be bang on. Now, as an adult I use this tool weekly.

The pendulum is limited to yes and no answers, so questions you ask must be phrased in that manner. Even with that limitation, the pendulum is a useful tool for a variety of purposes.

For example, many ghost hunters use pendulums to detect spirit presence, interdimensional portals and energy vortexes that may be present in a haunted location. The pendulum can be used to divine water, or find a lost object. For missing objects, a series of questions of elimination would need to be asked. Psychics who work on crime cases use pendulums over maps to find the location of missing persons and bodies, and murder weapons that have been hidden or disposed of.

We recommend that everyone own a pendulum and experiment with it. It will help you to open up psychically, and will teach you to trust when the information is on the nail.

You can find beautiful pendulums online or in spiritual stores, or you can make your own. Some are made of ornate crystals such as amethyst, clear quartz or moonstone, and others are made of copper or brass. Some are carved of wood. Whatever the material, the pendulum should have enough weight so that it hangs well at the end of its cord, and is not easily manipulated.

To start, you need to condition or train the pendulum by asking it to show you a yes answer and a no answer. The motions will not necessarily be the same for everyone, but they should be clear to you. It may take some time for the pendulum to become responsive.

Experienced dowsers develop their own techniques. You may have seen a dowser with a pendulum rotating with great vigor, and it looks like they are swinging it with their hand. This is not the case. Some of them get a "feel" for how the pendulum is responding, and a great deal of energy rushes through the arm and hand.

Pendulums can help validate your intuition and psychic flashes, and thus bolster the trust you have in your ability and in the accuracy of the information you receive.

CHAPTER 10

GIVING READINGS

Now that you've applied yourself to all the exercises so far, your hard work and dedication will start to show as you embark on doing readings for others. It's quite natural to feel a little nervous at giving readings in the beginning. That's a good sign, as it shows you want to do a good job! It's the most wonderful feeling reuniting loved ones and friends with those who have crossed over.

Below are the types of mediumistic readings you can do for others. It can take time to settle into the role of medium, but with the 'Three P's' we discussed in Chapter 1 – patience, practice and perseverance – you will soon find your ground.

Types of Readings

Private readings

In a private reading, which is sometimes called a consultation or sitting, the medium will sit with one person or perhaps a family, depending on the circumstances. The purpose is to connect them with their loved ones and guides, and bring through messages and good evidence. The sitters should have no doubt who they are communicating with, and this is why detailed evidence is important. It's not enough to say, 'I have a lady here with grey hair'. That is far too general, vague, and open to wide interpretation. You need to peel the onion and deepen the connection with specific details.

Both medium and sitters should feel as though they are in a special bond with spirit during the reading. This is a sacred time for everyone to experience first-hand the miracle of life-after-death communication.

A private reading is a more informal, relaxed affair than readings given in a development circle or platform demonstration.

Development circle readings

Most, but not all, mediums at one time or another have sat in a development circle. A development circle is where a group of like-minded individuals come together for the mutual development of mediumship. You literally sit in a circle, which helps the continuous flow of energy. It's also nice to be able to see people and their reactions around the circle.

Many spiritual shops, holistic centres and Spiritualist churches will offer development classes. We ourselves run development circles and love teaching people.

If you should wish to talk and develop your mediumship with like-minded people, search for a suitable group. It's a great way to develop confidence and accuracy for giving spirit messages. In a good circle, everyone should be supportive, as you are all in the same boat, there to develop. It doesn't matter how long some may have been attending; some more experienced sitters are happy to share their experiences.

Finding the right group dynamic is important. Above all, make sure you feel comfortable, as this will help you relax and unfold at a much quicker rate.

As we've said, not all mediums have sat in development circles. We know a few professional mediums who never found the right group for them. They sat at home, as you have been doing with spirit, and were guided by them. They are very fine mediums.

So, whether you decide to sit alone to develop, have a few friends round for a circle, or go to a more formalised development circle, the choice is up to you. You can do all three. Just make sure you go with what feels right for you.

Gallery or platform readings

In gallery or platform readings, a medium usually stands on a stage or platform before a large audience and is guided by spirit to select certain individuals for messages. Only some of the people will be selected from the audience. The messages are shorter than those given in a private reading (or even development circle), but the accuracy of messages demonstrates to everyone in the audience the presence of spirit. As we said previously, it's the quality of the message, not the quantity that is evidential.

Some mediums say they pick subjects by a light they see hovering over their heads, or they just 'feel' drawn to someone. Some mediums throw out a general question and ask who might relate to it, and then select from the individuals who raise their hands. It may be customary in some places for the medium to ask permission, such as, 'May I come to you'?

Understandably, some people avoid big group readings because they are embarrassed by the prospect of being picked from the crowd. It may be that they are unsure how they will react emotionally to the message. We've seen all sorts of emotions come out during a message, from sheer joy to anger. Most people, however, are happy to receive a message.

One-on-One Practice

It can be daunting to stand up in front of a group with all eyes on you, knowing the audience has high expectations. That can seem like a lot of pressure. You are not just reading for a few individuals – you are performing for the entire crowd. Before you undertake a large audience, practice doing as many one-on-one readings you can. This will help you gain the confidence you need to stand up before an audience. The exception for larger groups is the development circle, which enables you to practice before a group in a safe and non-judgemental environment.

Depending on how much you practice, it can take quite a while to become proficient at doing one-on-one readings. To cite an oft-used phrase, 'practice makes perfect'.

A professional private reading usually lasts 30 to 60 minutes on average. However, some will offer shorter readings at fayres and events. In the beginning, go with the flow and see how long your reading may last. As you become more accustomed to giving readings, you will find that you will need at least 30 minutes once information begins to flow. It is best not to charge a fee for your practice readings. It is a good idea to have the client give you feedback, so you can see how your journey of mediumistic development is shaping up.

Sitters

Friends are excellent sitters or clients for practice. Most will bite your hand off if you offer them a free reading. Tap people you do not know well to minimise projection of information you know about someone. This also prevents someone from saying, 'Well, you already knew that'.

Most friends are supportive and want to help you succeed. Ask them to be honest with their responses, and make sure they vocalise their response. The vibration and tone of the sitter's voice contributes to the strength of the link to spirit. We always ask to hear a sitter's voice, and it's a good habit for you to get into as well. A mere nod or shake of the head is simply not a valid way for a sitter or client to acknowledge the medium during spirit communication.

You should also practice reading for total strangers. You will have no prior knowledge of them or their circumstances; therefore, the evidence is powerful for you both. Some people freeze at the thought of reading for strangers. If you are going to become a professional medium or at least an accomplished one, you need to get past that anxiety, for most of your initial client base may consist of people you do not know.

In the beginning, you will probably prefer to read in person. At some point, expand to readings by telephone. You should be able to tune in to the voice of the sitter in order to make the bridge to the spirit world. Readings by phone are excellent practice, because you will not have any subtle response clues such as facial expressions and body language to give you information.

Whomever you choose for practice, verify that they are open-minded about mediumship and thus open to possibilities of making a connection with spirit. A closed person with a cynical attitude can sour the whole experience, which won't be of any help to you.

The reading

Select appointment times when you will not be rushed to finish in order to do something else. The more relaxed you are the stronger the connection. Spirit are always ahead of us, though, and they know who needs to be there for the client.

Allow an hour or so, which is plenty of time for the reading and follow-up conversation.

We advise getting yourself 'in the zone' before a reading. Use one of the techniques you have learned in this book to get rid of distracting thoughts and clear your mind. We are often asked if one should mediate before every reading, but it is not necessary. For us, getting into the zone means to close our eyes and breathe deeply for a couple of minutes, and then say a prayer, affirmation or invocation to send out a signal to the spirit world.

Here is the basic format for a reading:

- Get into the zone, switch on, open your chakras, breathe and affirm.

- Sit opposite your client. If you wish, take their hand for a minute to get a good energetic rapport.

- Mentally ask spirit to come, sit and wait for the connection. When you feel it, begin talking and say whatever comes to you.

- When you feel spirit move away, say this to the client.

- Turn off the switch and close the reading with thanks to spirit.

Now is the time for feedback. Ask the client for their comments and evaluation. If the sitter has said no to any piece of information, or is unsure, ask them to clarify with some other family member and to let you know the outcome.

Gathering and building evidence

Trainee mediums often ask us during our workshops, 'What sort of evidence are we looking to get in a message from the spirit world'?

Below we have compiled a 10-point checklist of things you should try to get from the communicating spirit. You can use this as a template if you wish. This helps you as the medium to give as much detailed evidence as possible to your clients.

Not every reading will necessarily have to cover all the points. The checklist provides a structure with which to work. In time and with more experience you will find you don't need such a checklist, as it all happens quite naturally. Just ask the spirit person silently, clear the mind and await the response. Trust the first thing you get. 'Spirit speaks first, you speak second!'

Evidence from Spirit Checklist

1. **Sex**: Is the spirit person a male or female? Even though we can be either sex throughout reincarnations, we need to know the sex of the spirit person in their last incarnation, so that they can be recognized. Ask them how they passed from this world, notice any sensations and describe what you are feeling. Did they have physical ailments that would be recognisable to the sitter?

2. **Names**: What names do you sense, hear, see or know that are associated with the communicating spirit or sitter receiving the message? Aim for first and surnames and wait for the response. If it doesn't come straight away move on, and it may follow.

3. **Physical traits**: Did they have a scar, birthmark, tattoo or other physical definition that stood out? Are they wearing noticeable jewellery? Perhaps you can see what clothing they liked to wear, note colours etc.

4. **Personality**: What sort of personality did they have? Quiet? Grumpy, or perhaps eccentric?

5. **Dates**: Are there any relevant dates that come to you, such as birthday, date of passing, anniversaries, or times of year or holidays that were important to them?

6. **Relationships**: Have they met anyone in spirit that they knew in life that would be recognisable to the sitter?

7. **Shared memories**: Are there some special memories that the client will understand, such as a holiday, wedding, party or birth you all shared?

8. **Place details**: What are descriptions of places, perhaps their home or neighbourhood or names of places that are relevant?

9. **Purpose**: Why have they come and what is their message? It could be just to visit and give their love or to reminisce. Perhaps they have some guidance or information they wish to impart?

10. **Awareness**: What earthly events has the spirit person witnessed or known since their passing that demonstrate to the sitter they are still aware of what's happening with their loved ones on earth?

Use this checklist especially during your early stages of development, as it will prove invaluable and will ensure that you cover as much ground as possible evidence-wise. Our students have used this structure for many years and give in-depth readings that are deeply meaningful. You may want to add a few other things to check off. It's all about making it work for you as an individual.

CHAPTER 11

CONDUCTING A SÉANCE

The time for the big event has arrived! You have read and put into practice the exercises in this book and now you feel ready to host your first séance – a gathering of people (three or more) to communicate with spirits on the other side through the agency of a medium. That's *you*.

You've seen in Chapter 2 the two main categories of mediumship practised in readings and séances, which are mental mediumship and physical mediumship. Most mediums, as we've noted, practice mental mediumship. However, sitters during a séance always love experiencing physical phenomena such as raps and table tipping. Many also seem to enjoy using spirit tools such as the trumpet, pendulum or Ouija board.

Review Chapter 2 if necessary. Below we guide you through the preparations for your very own séance. These points may seem like common sense, but it is surprising how often important factors are overlooked.

Séance Checklist

Plan your event

Decide how you want your séance to work. What kinds of activities do you want to try? Are you all going to sit quietly and ask for spirit to make their presence known? Do you want to use spirit communication tools such as a spirit board? Do you want to see undisputable physical evidence from spirit such as using table tipping? Seeing a table tilt or on occasion levitate is quite a sight to behold, and certainly shows a strong manifestation from spirit.

Think about how you want to host this séance and what you feel comfortable doing and using (as opposed to catering to expectations). You don't have to go all out and use all tools that are available, especially if this is your first séance or you have not yet had much experience running one. In time, you will find what works best for you and your group. Experiment. You may find that table tipping works well with certain individuals and not with others, or that the attendance of a particular sitter helps boost the energy in the room for stronger, clearer signals from spirit.

What you include in your séance, and how many people can attend, will be affected by the space you have available.

The venue

Some mediums are fortunate to have a facility or home that lends itself to a séance. However, just about any place can be converted to the right ambience, whether it's a new house or condo, or even a hotel meeting room.

Séances held in haunted places or on sacred sites are always popular – people feel they will have a greater chance of spirit contact, or perhaps even a spectacular display of phenomena. Energy of place is a significant factor to consider.

A gathering of people for the purpose of communicating with the spirit world is often referred to as a séance.

Haunted locations may sound glamorous, but their energy needs to be carefully evaluated. Many haunted sites are famous for their negative activity – not the kind of place where you want to open up to spirit. Nonetheless, some mediums are hired to conduct séances in such places for paranormal investigators and others as entertainment.

Sacred sites are renowned for their spiritual power. They are places where people go to contact spirits and the gods, so to speak. Some of them have usage restrictions. If you have the opportunity to hold a séance at or near a sacred site, count yourself lucky.

Most mediums make use of private homes – sometimes their own – and other facilities, and hold very successful séances. The medium and the sitters are the most important factors.

Setting the stage

Creating the most conducive atmosphere for a séance is vital to its success. Most of us have some preconceived ideas about séance trappings. Will there be a huge antique oak dining table with a Liberace-style candelabra adorning it? Will the room be dimly lit with only candlelight casting shadows? Or will it be like an ordinary living room at home?

Any comfortable room can be used and staged for the perfect atmosphere. Attendees should feel relaxed in an inviting setting. Avoid using a room starkly lit by a huge luminescent tube. Soft and dim light helps sitters get in 'the zone'. Avoid or clean up rooms with clutter, such as piles of newspapers and magazines strewn about, and rooms full of stale cigarette smoke or last night's curry.

Eliminate distractions. You might love your pets and feel they should be part of the séance, but they can be a nuisance to the sitters, especially if they wander in and out and jump up on people or furniture for attention. If there are other occupants of the home who will not be participating, encourage them to be away for a few hours. The noises of someone moving around in another part of the house, flushing a toilet, running water, and so on, will be disruptive. Above all, no one should play a radio or television, or cook food.

As the séance organiser, you need to ensure that people attending get taken out of the mundane world and into that atmospheric spirit world, and feel anticipation and excitement at the possibilities the séance holds. When you look around your home for a suitable spot, ask yourself what you will need to do to suitably alter the environment. It doesn't need to be Hollywood elaborate, for even small touches – a dark mirror, exotic candles, a fringed velvet throw or pillow – can set the stage.

With a little thought and imagination, you can create the right ambience. It doesn't matter if you live in a brand-new house or condo or a gothic-style mansion dating back to the 1600s. A few creative touches and your séance will prove to be a most enlightening and exciting evening.

We often host séances in our own home. We do not have a room exclusively used for séances, and so we use either our living room or dining room, depending on the numbers attending.

We stage our home for the séance in a simple, yet effective way. Our décor already reflects our spirituality, so we are half way there. We make use of our dining chairs for people who wish to sit up taller, and for those attending with any physical ailments we ensure that a comfortable armchair is available. The lights are soft – we use small lamps. We also ensure that there is enough space for air to circulate.

It can get very hot during a séance with energy that is raised so we have started using a few battery-operated candles, so not to add to the heat. It is also safer if people start moving around for toilet breaks. One central real flame candle is used for the centre, to illuminate the circle from within. This gives subtle light so the sitters can see what is happening at all times. It is also advantageous, as we've found that this candle, which we light in honour to the spirit world, can draw spirit near, very quickly. The candle can also be a good indicator of sudden spirit breezes. Ensure the candle is secure in place; a hurricane lantern is a good idea.

Time and length

A séance can be held during the day or evening. Most people prefer to do séances at night. For a daytime séance, select a room where sunlight can be shut out or reduced.

How long it should last will depend on many factors. You may be limited by the availability of the facility or room. Group dynamics are another factor to consider – how long do you think your sitters will be able to hold and focus their attention?

It may take a while to get the energy going. As you are starting out, the minimum séance length should be 30 minutes. As you get more experience, you can extend them to fit you and the group.

Work up to 30 minutes and then gauge how it's flowing. If the séance is proving to be very active, then continue. Sometimes you may get to 30 minutes and find that you have had some form of spirit contact and that is enough, so you and the group can stop there if you wish to.

You need to establish with your sitters before you start that the length of the séance will depend on the energy and spirit activity.

Lunar phases

Whether people want to believe it or not, the moon plays an integral part in augmenting powerful energies for all kinds of spiritual activities – paranormal, healing and magical, in addition to spirit communication. If you pay attention to lunar phases, you may start to notice distinct patterns in séance activity and results. For example, paranormal investigators know that both the new moon and full moon nights are the most active, with high activity also falling a day or two before and after.

Many people know folk beliefs about the moon being at 'full power' when it is full, but why is the new moon such an active night? Perhaps it has to do with a restart of the lunar phase cycle, an 'empty' time during which fresh lunar energies begin their flow.

The moon waxes and wanes in a 28-day cycle. During the waxing stage from new to full, lunar energy is gaining power. In folklore, the waxing moon is a good time for activities intended for increase and gain. The lunar power peaks at the full moon. Seances held on this night (or a night before or after) can be quite powerful.

During the waning phrase from full to new, the lunar power decreases. You can still conduct an effective séance during this time, however. Symbolically, the waning phase is good for elimination, letting go and endings. Mentally focus on eliminating doubt and obstacles to spirit communication for your sitters. Perhaps the séance can help a sitter let go of grief. New moon séances can mark the beginning of something significant for the sitters. These are associations you can discuss with your sitters at the start.

If you are renting a place for a séance, or conducting one as part of a conference or a tour, you will not always be able to choose your timing according to the lunar calendar. Just take that into account. Lunar phase calendars are available online.

Power days

Power days are times of seasonal change: the solstices, equinoxes and midpoints. They can be useful in planning a séance.

In pagan times, the changing of the seasons had great significance, and many folk customs arose to take advantage of the seasonal energies with great festivals. The festivals were honoured or observed by all our ancestors, primarily with rituals intended to foster fertility of crops and livestock. Many of these festivals have now been modernized or adapted to fit religions or specific cultures. These change of season days are still just as powerful as they ever have been. They are excellent times to hold séances.

The most famous power day for spirit communication is Halloween, also known by its Celtic name Samhain (pronounced SOW-in, from an old Irish word meaning 'summers end'). It has a long history of being the time of year when the veil between the worlds is the thinnest, and spirits can come into the land of the living.

The summer and winter solstices have always been important power days, with many festivals and rites, especially involving bonfires. After that are the spring and fall equinoxes, and then some mid-season power days, such as mid-winter and the time of harvest. In earlier times, Beltane reigned as a major day, celebrated by fire festivals to mark the blossoming of life.

Below is a list of major power days with their most commonly observed dates. Candlemas is taken from the Gaelic (Imbolc) observance of the beginning of spring. Beltane is a fertility rite festival. Lughnasadh/Lammas (Gaelic and Old English terms, respectively) derives from harvest festivals.

The first dates are for the Northern Hemisphere (NH) followed by the dates for the Southern Hemisphere (SH). We have included old and traditional names as well.

Halloween (Samhain) – October 31 (NH) April 30-May 1 (SH)

Winter solstice (Yule) – On or around December 21 (NH) June 21 (SH)

Candlemas (Imbolc) – February 1-2 (NH) August 1 (SH)

Spring equinox (Ostara) – On around March 21 (NH) September 21 (SH)

Beltane – April 30- May 1 (NH) October 31 (SH)

Summer solstice (Litha) – On or around June 21 (NH) December 21 (SH)

Lughnasadh/Lammas – August 1 (NH) February 2 (SH)

Autumn equinox (Mabon)—On or around September 21 (NH) March 21 (SH)

If you have the planning flexibility, is it better to choose a lunar phase or a power day? They both have their advantages. If you are lucky enough to find that you have a good moon phase and a power day on the same date you can tap into an even more intense energy. Personally, we have found that the most amazing times for séances or mediumship are Halloween and Beltane.

If you are interested in taking advantage of power days, we recommend you do some research of their histories and traditions. Some of their elements can be incorporated into your séance.

Select a leader

The séance leader is someone who is advanced in knowledge and has mediumistic gifts, but may not yet be a working medium. This person will lead the group in the opening prayer or setting of sacred space. The leader will do all the asking of questions to the spirits during the séance. This prevents sitters from talking over each other, and keeps order. The leader also closes the séance and thanks the spirits for attending.

You should select your leader in advance of the séance. Announce it during the orientation.

Attendees

Plan your guest list carefully to include calm and level-headed people you know you can trust. Trust in the early stages is important. You want to know that everything that happens is genuine, and having trusted sitters helps you achieve this.

The ideal guests should be as intrigued to experience the wonders of spirit as you are, and are open-minded to the whole experience. Having cynical, close-minded sceptics will not create the right atmosphere and can alienate the other sitters and prevent spirit from attending at all. Why would spirit want to come to a séance when someone is being churlish? We avoid situations like that in our daily lives. In fact, we probably wouldn't want to come back from spirit ourselves for ill-tempered people.

Another thing to ensure is that all the sitters are truly ready for this session and that they are not quietly terrified at the prospect of spirit manifesting. Pre-screen your sitters with an honest dialogue. It's quite normal for the inexperienced and newcomers to feel a little apprehensive, but those who are going to quietly fret and be a bundle of nerves should not attend, as they will impede the flow of the séance. It's all about respect for all the sitters, yourself as medium, and, of course, spirit. So, ensure your list of prospective sitters is thoroughly thought out.

Ask your sitters not to wear perfumes or colognes, which may mask paranormal smells or contaminate evidence. For example, if you are communicating with a spirit who tries to manifest through the smell of flowers or lavender, those smells can be overridden by perfume. If someone is wearing a floral or lavender scent, it may be mistaken for evidence. There is also the hazard of allergic reactions among the sitters, or reactions of distaste. What pleases one person may repel another.

Tell your attendees that they must arrive promptly and that any late comers will not be permitted entrance. This may sound strict, especially if someone gets stuck in traffic, but this too is in the interest of all participants. Once the session has begun with a brief chat, the entrance of someone who is flustered from trying to park can upset the balance of the room. Post a sign on your outside door saying that session has begun and there is no admittance. Make sure that everyone understands this in advance, and that those who anticipate delays of any kind should allow extra travel time. Better to be early than late.

Give everyone a brief orientation at the start. Tell them what the order of service will be. For example, are you all going to meditate first, and who will lead the prayer or affirmation of protection? Are you all going to sit and see what happens, or are you going to employ tools such table tipping or the spirit board?

Also, something that many people overlook is, what to wear. Advise your sitters to dress for comfort, not fashion. For example, we like wearing slim fit jeans, but if we're sitting down for long periods or leaning across a spirit board, we find they can be very restrictive. Suggest relaxed clothing with an expanding waist, and a sweater or shawl in case of an unexpected chill. Keep those close by so as not to disturb the session.

It's quite common for the temperature in the room to go up and down during a séance regardless of the thermostat setting. Temperature fluctuations can have you sweating or feeling chilly – and sometimes both in the same session. To start, the séance room should not be overly hot or cold. If you can, prevent a central heating system from repeatedly going on and off. Some systems can create noises, pops and creaks, which may be misinterpreted as spirit activity.

Bathroom breaks

Bathroom breaks are at your discretion, depending on how long the séance lasts. A break for people to get up will also break the energy in the room. If you plan no break, advise everyone of that at the start and give them time to use the facilities.

Of course, there are times when a person just has to go. You can also announce in your orientation that if such a situation arises, please be as quiet as possible. Or, you can plan for a break, and let everyone know there will be one. You will need to re-establish the energy in the room – or, it may be a good time to switch activities, such as experimenting with table tipping.

Offerings

Offerings are a practice we have seen overlooked by many groups. Once they have introduced this to their practice on our guidance they have found it to be beneficial. It's always nice to receive a gift, and spirits are no different. Remember that we are looking to communicate with spirits who have lived a human existence. If they have made the effort to come to the séance, it is appropriate to offer them a small gift, such as flowers, spring water, milk or honey. An offering does not guarantee the attendance of any spirit, but it is a nice respectful way of giving thanks.

One medium I (Stuart) knew who was 30 years my senior always said that offerings would not make a difference. I asked him if there was ever someone who passed over that he had never heard from and was surprised by that. He said yes, his father, to whom he was close.

I asked him what was the one thing that he remembered that his dad loved. He answered, 'Cigars'. I suggested that he bring a cigar to a séance (unlit of course) and offer it to his father silently during the opening prayer. After 10 minutes, people were aware of the smell of cigar smoke in the room – it was coming from the wrapped cigar inside his jacket. To the medium's surprise, his dad came through loud and clear with details only he knew. Evidently dad enjoyed his cigar!

He called me the next day and excitedly told me that he heard from his dad. He was on top of the world. He admitted how wrong he had been and said, 'You can still teach an old dog new tricks'.

Filming

With the advent of smart phones, it's safe to say that most of us have a camera or recording device on our mobile phones. Some people ask us if they can take video footage during the séance with their phone and our answer is always NO. The reason for this is very simple. If your cell phone is being used as a video recorder it means your phone is switched on and able to receive text messages, calls and updates from social media and other apps. During the séance, all phones, without exception, must be turned off, and that means powered off, not just switched to silence. There is nothing more disrespectful to the sitters and the visiting spirits than to have a phone suddenly vibrate. Even if the phone is on silent and doesn't vibrate, it is an intrusive energy that can disrupt the balance of the energy in the room, and can stop communication with the other side.

Filming a séance takes away from the special sacred connection we have with the spirit world. Also, not every sitter wants to be filmed taking part in a séance. It is an invasion of privacy. Most important, spirit don't always want to show up in video. If your great aunt Fanny used to loathe being on camera and would shy away at the prospect, is she going to come to a filmed séance?

Having said that, we have filmed some séances, but only during paranormal investigations with permission from the sitters and of course, spirit. This is for our personal use only, to assist in research and the gathering of evidence.

If all your sitters are happy to be filmed, and you invite the spirits that are happy to come forth when filming is commenced and assure them the séance is not a dog and pony show, then you may very well have the success we have had.

146

You must decide what to do with the footage if phenomena are caught. Will you keep it for your own records or share it publicly? This must be agreed upon by the group before the séance begins.

Assessing the evidence

Keep detailed records of all your seances, noting the things that worked well and what did not. Solicit evaluations and feedback from your sitters. Some séances will produce a great deal of activity and others will not. Note any patterns and consistent characteristics. Fine tune your process.

Where do you go from here?

Congratulations! By now you have learned a great deal about mediumship and your own ability. You know your strengths, and you know what you need to improve. The skill of mediumship is never really finished – it's an ongoing process of learning and development that gets richer and richer as you go along. We absolutely love our work!

You probably also by now have a good idea what you want to do with your mediumship. Perhaps your desire to become a professional is stronger. Perhaps you've decided that you want to keep it a more personal pursuit, something you do with friends and family. Either path is a winner – you have been brought into closer contact with the spirit world, and your life has changed for the better as a result.

This book is an introduction to this wonderful field, a door-opener. You have started an amazing journey, and we wish you love and blessings along your way.

Contact the Authors

Stuart

Stuart is a well-respected international psychic medium, paranormal investigator and healer who works closely with the spirit world and angels. Stuart has always been aware of their presence since childhood and as he grew older he knew his life's mission was to work alongside them.

Stuart studied with renowned medium and teacher, Glyn Edwards at the famous Arthur Findlay college in London. He has appeared on national and international television and on radio, He also appeared on the hit TV series *Come dine with me*, casting a spell with the dinner party guests.

Stuart's warmth, compassion and accuracy, combined with his down-to-earth approach, has drawn clients from across the world, making him a much sought-after psychic practitioner.

Dean

Dean is a popular and respected psychic medium, healer, paranormal investigator and spiritual practitioner. His development took him to the world-renowned Arthur Findlay College in London, England with medium Glyn Edwards, who was one of the world's finest and respected mediums and teachers.

He has appeared on TV, radio and in the news. His grounded approach to his work, combined with his compassion, accuracy and humour, attracts people from every walk of life and making him much sort after. He loves to share his wealth of knowledge through his writing and workshops.

149

Stuart and Dean have been working together since 1995 when they first met. They formed a strong bond and knew they had lived many past lives together. Both having had spiritual experiences from childhood, they realised the divine had put them together. They are 'soul mates'.

Their interest in the spiritual field has grown with them, experiencing delights of what working with spirit truly holds. They have regular trips across the UK and USA to places of spiritual power, be it Stonehenge, Avebury, Glastonbury, Salem, Massachusetts or Sedona, Arizona. These trips enrich the work they do and brings further blessing to all who seek their guidance.

They live in Shakespeare's beautiful county of Warwickshire, England in a spiritual home with a few happy spirits.

Stuart and Dean offer a wide range of spiritual and healing services, including mediumship, angel and Tarot readings; mentoring programs; paranormal investigation services; enchanted parties; Reiki, aura cleansing and other healing services; spirit circles; and classes and workshops.

Make bookings and sign up for their free e-newsletter at:
www.stuartanddean.com